29 Da

Smooth Move

29 Days to a Smooth Move

2nd Edition

- ✓ Save Your Cents
- ✓ Save Your Sanity
- ✓ Save Scads of Your Time

Written and published by
Donna Kozik & Tara Maras

iUniverse, Inc.
New York Lincoln Shanghai

29 Days to a Smooth Move
2nd Edition

iUniverse books may be ordered through booksellers or by contacting:

iUniverse
2021 Pine Lake Road, Suite 100
Lincoln, NE 68512
www.iuniverse.com
1-800-Authors (1-800-288-4677)

All product names and/or logos are copyrights and trademarks of their respective owners. None of these owners has authorized, sponsored, endorsed or approved this publication. *29 Days to a Smooth Move* has not received any remuneration in return for including the name of any company or product in this book.

The authors and publishers, Donna Kozik and Tara Maras of Marik Communications LLC, have made their best effort to produce a high quality, informative and helpful book. But they make no representation or warranties of any kind with regard to the completeness or accuracy to its contents. They accept no liability of any kind for any losses or damages caused or alleged to be caused, directly or indirectly, from using the information contained in this book.

ISBN-13: 978-0-595-35957-8 (pbk)
ISBN-13: 978-0-595-80408-5 (ebk)
ISBN-10: 0-595-35957-4 (pbk)
ISBN-10: 0-595-80408-X (ebk)

Printed in the United States of America

29 Days to a Smooth Move

Long (and Short) Distance Dedications

We dedicate this book to those who supported us in our cross country moves—whether it was by helping seek out the "good" boxes, taking valuable but bulky items off our hands or providing a shoulder to lean on during those stressful days.

From Donna:

To Daniel, for being my friend and seeding my mind with the magic words: "I'm moving to San Diego—and I think you should, too."

To Teresa, for being the best sister ever and for knowing when to say, "It's not 'if' you're moving, it's 'when!'"

From Tara:

To Ron, for being the best "travelin' buddy" a girl could ask for on the road and through our journey through life as partners. Your endless support and love mean the world to me.

To Mom and Dad, for encouraging me to chase my dreams. Whether it was selling painted rocks as a kid, mowing through my teens, typing through college, honeymooning on eBay profits or writing this book—you never doused my entrepreneurial spirit!

Thinking about getting married in Las Vegas?

Look for *The Las Vegas Wedding Advisor*, Donna and Tara's next book, to be published in Spring 2006. From chapels to dresses to transportation, *The Las Vegas Wedding Advisor* is your personal wedding consult to the ins and outs of saying "I do" in Las Vegas.

Find out more at **lasvegasweddingadvisor.com**

Contents

Bonus Sections

How To Use This Book

Congratulations! With *29 Days to a Smooth Move,* you are well on your way to a hassle-free relocation!

This is your personal moving manual. In fact, *29 Days to a Smooth Move* is your go-to resource for the entire adventure.

We Assume...

> You've already made the decision to move, and you know where in the world you're heading!
>
> This is a major move and you want to make the best use of your time.

We *know* that *you know* you need to pack, sell your home, find movers, clean out—but that you're not quite sure *how* to prioritize your time and your tasks.

We Also Think...

> **You want to save money in the process.** We'll show you how to trim the fat from your moving expenses and outline the costs you can expect, down to the final roll of packing tape.
>
> **You want to think like an expert.** Think of this book as a crash course in Moving 101. You have just enough information to be dangerous, and you'll be thinking like the pros in no time. We arm you with critical "must ask" questions. Plus, with Tara's Tales and Donna's Ditties—our personal stories sprinkled throughout—you'll avoid the mistakes we made and learn from our successes.
>
> **You are a bit overwhelmed!** It's no secret that moving is one of life's most stressful events. Put away the Alka Seltzer because this book is chock full of step-by-step instructions, planning calendars, checklists and everything you'll need for a smooth and easy move.

Whatever Works for You

The best part about this book is that it's easy to skip around. With our "Make a Moving Memo" and "Make a Date" reminders, there's plenty of room for you to jot down notes and keep track of your own information. So, start at the beginning or get a nagging topic out of the way early in the process. You can always come back later to learn more.

Looking For Something Specific?

Zoinks! You say you have fewer than 29 days? Cruise ahead to *Chapter 2: Movers or Me?* when you're deciding whether to hire movers or do it yourself.

Is your timeline more flexible? Start with *Chapter 1: Getting a Grip on Your Time* and structure a moving plan with our scheduling and time management tips before working your way through *29 Days to a Smooth Move.*

If you're moving on a shoestring, check out *Section 2: Save Your Cents* where you'll learn about the expected costs and how Uncle Sam can save you some cash.

Need help sorting out the nightmare that is your house? Groove on over to *Chapter 9: Sort It Out Before You Pack It Up,* and we'll teach you what to pack, how to pack, when to pack...and how to avoid lighting yourself and your moving van on fire!

Prepared to push the pets into their carriers? Terrified about telling your boss? Kids killing you with stress? We've got the answers to all that, too. *Section 5: Save Your Sanity* is all about keeping yourself centered during the chaotic times.

We're a Team!

Have a problem and can't find the answer in this book? Discover a time-saving tactic you want to share with others in future editions? Just e-mail us at info@29daystoasmoothmove.com. We're online all the time and will get back to you promptly.

A Chat with the Authors:
Insights into the Art of Moving

We're sure you have a few questions right off the bat.

To get started and give you an idea of where we're coming from (and gone to!) here's some general moving information you need to know now—and where you can find the specifics in this book.

Q: What's the most important thing to keep in mind when conducting a "big move?"

Tara: First of all, don't be fooled. Any move where you can't stack your china in the back seat of the car and drive it safely to your new home in a matter of minutes (and without breaking a sweat) is a big move!

Whether across country or across town, moving is a huge deal. So it's important to treat it as such from the get go.

When my husband, Ron, and I made the decision to move from Erie, Pa. to Las Vegas, Nev., we got serious before we got packing.

On the night we committed to the move, we had an "offsite" planning meeting at the local Borders bookstore. Armed with a map, three-ring binder, calendar and two white mochas, we charted our course for the next two months. It was the beginning of our new beginning—and a great way to kickoff our adventure. I highly recommend an initial offsite meeting to map out your plans.

Read more about ways initial planning can reduce your moving stress in Chapter 1: Get a Grip on Your Time.

Donna: Above all, the key to a smooth move is *organization*. Being organized will bring

- ✓ focus in the midst of chaos
- ✓ calmness in the center of panic and
- ✓ hope in times of despair.

Didn't know moving would bring on more emotional drama than a daytime soap opera, did you?

Most of all, organization will help tame the procrastination beast. If you're like most folks, you have a tendency to put off until tomorrow (or next week or next month) what could be done today. Heck, I'm like that, and I managed to move over 2,000 miles from Erie to San Diego and keep my wits about me.

This book leads you to that light at the end of the tunnel. Follow our advice, and you will get your move done in good time and in good shape.

For more information about sorting your stuff out for a more organized move-out, go to Chapter 9: Sort It Out Before You Pack It Up.

Q: Why do you consider yourselves moving experts?

Tara: Ron and I made the decision to move across the country on May 2, 2001. We put our house on the market June 1, gave our employers two weeks' notice on June 15, logged off our computers for the last time on June 29 and drove out of Erie six days later.

In just 63 days, we managed to sell our home and a car, return every item we'd ever borrowed, pack six rooms, an attic, garage and basement, plan a cross-country trip, attend a half dozen gatherings in our honor and secure an apartment in Las Vegas. We lived to tell about it, and by following the tips and techniques in this book, you will live through your adventure as well!

Donna: Less than two years before I moved across the country, I first relocated from a 200-acre farm to a downtown apartment in Erie.

During both moves, I learned the benefits of having many, many, many boxes, several black markers and industrial-size rolls of bubble wrap. I also learned about the invigoration that comes with throwing things away, the importance of accepting help and the excitement of a fresh start.

But there's more to moving than changing a physical location—there are also some heavy-duty emotional aspects. It's important to get your grandmother's Waterford Crystal moved in one piece, but it's also vital to do some emotional work along with the physical work. Both Tara and I had our ups and downs with moving and will share our problems—and solutions—to help you with a smooth and easy emotional move!

Q: What did you find most intimidating about the moving process? How did you handle that?

Donna: For me, the most intimidating part was doing it all *myself.* Yes, I had supportive friends (like Tara) to help talk it up, pack it in and move it out, but there were plenty of times, usually late at night, where I had to dig deep and find the energy to keep on keeping on. In times of fear, I took a deep breath, gave myself a pep talk and reaffirmed why I decided to move and, yes, I could do it.

And, if nothing else, I repeated one saying that has seen me through much of life: This too shall pass!

Tara: Saying goodbye was the most emotional part of our moving experience. The daunting task of adequately bidding farewell to the only city we had ever lived in and to the friends and families that we loved so much was more difficult than packing, scheduling movers or selling our home. But, goodbyes are a necessary part of moving and, more often than not, you'll end up wet-faced. Chalk it up to part of the moving experience.

For more about learning how to say goodbye, go to Chapter 17: Saying Goodbye— It's a Family Affair.

Q: Was there one certain problem that threw you? What was it and how did you solve it?

Tara: I totally underestimated the time it would take to pack our house.

Although we packed almost everything ahead of time, we made the huge mistake of saving some of the most complicated items for the bitter end. On Moving Day Eve, we persevered through the night and worked harder than we ever had as a team, not letting tape dispenser injuries or our charged emotions get the better of us.

Donna: Pets present their own problems, and how I was going to move my three cats across the country was a big concern. Like most pet owners, I think of Bart, Baby and That Crazy Frisbee as family members. First I worried about how I was going to get them to California, and then I worried how they would react once they got there. The bottom line is that they were taken care of and arrived safe in San Diego. (And, by the way, they are extremely well adjusted cats.)

Go to Chapter 20: Moving the Whole "Kitten" Kaboodle (Or Poochie Patoodle!) *for more information about moving pets.*

Q: Is there one thing you kept in mind to help see you through the stressful times? What was it and how did it help you?

Tara: Moving is stressful, no doubt. Something will go wrong, so just expect it from the beginning. No matter how much you plan, pray and prepare for a glitch-free move, it just isn't going to happen. Anticipate at least one mini-disaster. Then, when it happens, you won't feel so discouraged, and you can cross it off your list!

When Ron and I moved, we quit our jobs, sold our house, said goodbye to our hometown, tearfully hugged the loved ones and set out on the open road for Las Vegas, a city we'd visited once and knew only from the Travel Channel. We were temporarily jobless, homeless, friendless and had only the clothes on our backs and our most meaningful material possessions in the trunk of our Honda Civic. Yet, somehow, it was the best time of our lives!

Donna: It seemed like the more hassles (albeit minor hassles, but still hassles) I encountered, the more determined I became to make my move and start a new beginning. Moving brings momentum to your life and can lead you to all kinds of invigorating changes. The thought of a fresh start kept me sane during all the stress that led up to it.

For more information about keeping your wits about you—or knowing where you packed them—see Chapter 16: An Ocean of Emotion.

Before we get on with the show, a couple more things.

Throughout *29 Days to a Smooth Move*, we'll be taking a time out here and there to share our personal experiences and tips: Tara's Tales and Donna's Ditties. We hope they provide valuable insight into how we handled our most challenging moving problems—so you can handle yours!

We've also included four bonus sections to help with your move and after you arrive at your new destination.

Bonus # 1: *29 Days to a Smooth Move* Calendar and Checklist
Reminders of nearly everything you have to do to move—complete in five pages.

Bonus # 2: *29 Days to a Smooth Move* Just the Facts
For the list makers among us, it's all of our "Make a Moving Memo" and "Make a Date" prompts in one section.

Bonus # 3: Make Your House a Home
A guide to unpacking—and unwinding—after your big adventure.

Bonus # 4: De-stress for New Success
A guide to taking care of mental and emotional needs after your move.

SECTION ONE

Save Scads of Your Time

This section of 29 Days to a Smooth Move *details how you can save time while planning, considering various moving options and exploring your new community.*

Chapter 1:
Get a Grip on Your Time
Plan now for a smooth move later. It's about taking an overwhelming project and making it more manageable.

What are the big jobs that you dread doing? What are the details you absolutely have to remember but have a funny feeling you'll forget? When's the last day of school? Who knows a reliable mover? Hey, does anybody have a pen?

Rest easy. This chapter will help you make the most of the time you have.

Chapter 2:
Should I Use Movers or Me?
One of the first decisions you have to make is whether to begin pumping iron so you can save some bucks by heaving your own boxes.

Or maybe you're going to hire movers who have spent years training for the upcoming triathlon of packing, moving and unpacking.

Or maybe it's something in between and you'll do the packing and someone else will do the lifting. Weigh your options and make your decision by using the information presented in this chapter.

Chapter 3:
Meet and Greet Your New Community
Getting to know you…getting to know all about you…

It's time to do some exploring! No doubt you have plenty of questions about where you're going and what you'll find once you get there.

Just as with all other aspects of moving life, organization and planning will serve you well here, too. Use this chapter's information to start uncovering your new community—and see what surprises are in store!

Chapter 1

Get a Grip on Your Time

29 days?!! It's going to take me 29 *years* to move all this stuff! No, 29 *decades*! No, 29 *eons*!

Okay, let's take a collective deep breath here.

Yes, you have a lot to do—but now is not the time for panic. As the saying goes, the longest journey begins with a single step, right? Well, your first vital step is making a plan now—so you can save time later!

Where will I find the time?

When you're looking to move in a hurry, you may have a sense of panic. There's so much to be done, and so little time to do it. You may even end up sitting around doing nothing at all, except worrying about how much you have to do!

We understand, because we've been there. And now we're here to share our experiences with you to make your move as smooth as possible (whether it's in 29 days—more or less).

The most important thing is to make a plan and stick with it. The second most important thing is to have faith in yourself and your abilities—the things that need to get done will get done.

You're going to get through this!

Avoid Procrastination

Time and energy you spend in putting off until the day before the movers arrive is time and energy you're going to wish you had back. Get up and get going now!

Who knows, you may even start to have some fun. Just think how good it will feel to be done ahead of schedule.

Donna's Ditty—

Memories—From the Corner of My Attic

When researching information for this book, I took a trip down memory lane and revisited my own moving manual, *California Bound!* It contains calendars, lists, resources, phone numbers, plans and dreams.

Use our book as your base for your smooth move, but try to make time to personalize your moving manual with quotes and pictures to inspire you, too!

Create a Master Resource

Luckily, with this book, this part is nearly done! Your moving manual will help the most unorganized soul stay focused. It will help the most hopeless procrastinator keep on track! It will leap tall boxes in a single bound, snatch small children from harm's way…

Okay, let's not get carried away. But we truly believe you will soon wonder how you ever could have moved without it! It's a good idea also to keep a folder or two alongside *29 Days to a Smooth Move* for those important papers that need to stay put instead of stray away.

Create a Master Plan

First, sit down with yourself or your family and review the general categories of the things that need to be done before your move. Don't worry about the details (they will come later), just the overall areas of your life that will need some attention, such as:

- ✓ Readying the house for new occupants
- ✓ Condensing your goods
- ✓ Packing your possessions

- ✓ Preparing the children
- ✓ Organizing paperwork, estimates, change of address forms, etc.
- ✓ Saying goodbye

 Make a Moving Memo

The "Big Picture" To-Do List
(Overall moving priorities from A to Z)

_____

_____

_____

_____

_____

_____

_____

_____

_____

_____

_____

Great! Now you have an idea of where to start.

Tara's Tale—

All's Right with Offsite

If your planning meeting consists of you and a spouse or partner, I encourage you to have it "offsite," in other words, away from the emotional center of your lives and the material surroundings that are your comfort zone. Think about the big picture, draft a timeline and write down some key dates.

Also, make a list of your reasons for moving and post it smack in the middle of your refrigerator. Every time your pass it, you'll be reminded of your goals and to-do list. (Next thing you know, you'll be loading that refrigerator onto the moving van!)

Break Down (and Divvy Up!) Tasks

After you have a list of everything that needs to be done, go back and create sub-lists.

We've done our best to help you by including "Make a Moving Memo" lists encompassing selling your home, packing, traveling to your new destination and everything in between. Add your own personal items and then let the worries go.

In addition to "Make a Moving Memo," we've also pulled out "Make a Date" lines you can fill in as you read and then coordinate on your moving calendar found in the back.

After all, the less "remembering" you have to do, the more energy you will have to concentrate on other aspects of your move.

Tara's Tale—

The Eviction

While I packed books and dishes, Ron took on the daunting task of cleaning out the garage. Our single-car garage consisted not only of garden-variety yard tools and paint cans, but something else—there was evicting to be done. Although we (well, actually Ron) dreaded it, it might as well be done sooner rather than later. That summer, we had planted new grass seed and used hay to deter the crows and wind from undoing our work. The spare hay bales found a home in our garage, and it wasn't long before every squirrel on Post Avenue had the same idea! (Don't worry, we gave them plenty of notice!)

Prioritize and Assign Time

After you have your lists ready, prioritize. What takes time and needs to be done first? What can wait until closer to the move? What has to be done during business hours? What can be done on the weekends? Use the time you do have to your best advantage.

Do a Little Every Day

Keep the pace to win the race! You'd be amazed what you can do if you focus for 60 minutes—the time of one talk show—a day. Consult your list of things to do and pick an area that appeals to you. Or pick an area that you dread doing. Or pick the biggest project. Whatever it is, make a pact to work 60 minutes straight at the project and watch progress unfurl before you.

Donna's Ditty—

Tonight At 11

I'll admit it: I love TV. Jay Leno, Dave Letterman and Ted Koppel watched me pack many a box. Others might prefer packing to music or even while doing silent meditation (very Zen).

Use Your Peak Energy Times

If you're a morning lark, get up an hour or two early to get some serious packing done before the day gets started. If you're a night owl, designate a time after most people are in bed to concentrate on your sorting and boxing. (And don't discount the energy provided by both growing enthusiasm and looming deadlines!)

Tackle the Big Projects First

Clean out the junk room. Get the overstuffed closets out of the way. Bring down everything from the attic. The longer you put these big projects off, the larger they will grow—especially in your mind!

 Make a Moving Memo

The things I dread doing—and when they will be done:

Task   Date for Completion

_____

_____

_____

_____

_____

_____

_____

_____

_____

_____

_____

Delegate and Solicit Help

Even if you're doing this solo and your friends are sorry to see you go, they will help you pack—don't be afraid to ask. (But if they are overly eager then, my friend, you have bigger problems.) It's amazing how much faster work gets done with four (Or six! Or eight!) hands instead of two.

Donna's Ditty—

She's One of a Kind!

It helps a great deal to have someone on your side who has to love you no matter how ugly you get. For me, that was my sister.

Without a complaint, Teresa helped me organize and pack for two big moves—no small feat, and, yes, I had my ugly moments! I simply could not have done it without her.

During this stressful time, take help when it's offered and don't be afraid to ask for help when you need it. And give yourself permission to lean a little on your close friends and family members.

 Make a Moving Memo

The friends who can help with sorting, packing and more:

_____

_____

_____

_____

_____

_____

Don't Sweat the Small Stuff

Sometimes it seems that the big decisions come easily and you can find yourself wasting precious minutes, or even hours, over something small. Watch out for these "time mines" working against you. When you find yourself stressing over something tiny, take a breath, save your sanity and move on. When you revisit the issue later you'll find it much easier to make the call.

A Place to Keep My Notes and Reminders…

Chapter 2

Should I Use Movers or Me?

The Reason for the Season

Sunshine, blue skies, no school…what could be better than a summertime move? If this is in your stars, it might be time to reconsider.

Did you know that June, July and August are the peak months in the moving industry? Sure, a summertime move reeks of convenience and ease when stacked up against the other options, and the elements that go along with them. It's these very moving conditions paired with the fact that a summertime move won't disrupt kids' school schedules that draw so many people to ship out in the sunshine.

And, regardless of the season, expect movers and rental trucks to book up fast at the beginning and end of each month. If you can stand to wait until the off season, you'll probably save some bucks because the American Moving and Storage Association says some companies offer discounts between October and April. Cha-ching!

Now you're probably thinking, "Are they suggesting I move on a Wednesday in the middle of January?" Well, we can almost guarantee that you'd pay less and be able to book later, but with some good planning you too can join June's migrating masses.

Tara's Tale—

Hot Fun in the Summertime

When we made the decision to move from Erie to Las Vegas, timing was everything.

We had one simple goal…get out of Erie before we had to turn on the furnace. If you know anything about lake effect weather, that meant vacating before the calendar turned to October. It was a snap to prepare our home for showing and selling in the sunshine.

Leaving Erie on July 5 was ideal. With sunny skies overhead and a few t-shirt changes tucked in our duffel bags, we scooted out of town before 4th of July tourists had even opened their eyes.

How did we avoid the headaches of a summer move? Book early. Book early. Book early!

Know Your Pros

Before you entrust the accumulation of your life's possessions to Mack's Marvelous Movers, there are several points to consider.

First, is Mack trustworthy? Look for the DOT. No, not Mack's tattoo. We're talking about the Department of Transportation license that you should find hanging in Mack's front office.

Don't see the DOT? Then bank on the bureau. Did Mack make the Millers mad? Call your local Better Business Bureau to see if there were any attacks filed against Mack.

How long has Mack been in business? Did Mack's dad, Zack, start the business decades ago? Is Mack licensed and bonded? Is Mack a hack or does he have the knack to get the job done?

Okay, okay, enough of the Dr. Seuss. The bottom line is that your time will be well spent shopping around and getting at least three estimates from reputable companies.

And remember, there's nothing as valuable as a referral from a friend or relative. If Mack put a smile on the face of your hard-to-please Uncle Jack, chances are he'll get the job done right for you!

 Make a Moving Memo

The pros I know and their phone numbers:

_____

_____

_____

_____

_____

_____

_____

_____

_____

It Pays To Ask

You wouldn't purchase a new car or put a down payment on a home without asking questions, would you? Signing the dotted line on a mover's contract is no different. The investment can be huge and since you'll be trusting strangers with the accumulation of your life's possessions, the stakes are high! Like any other major purchase, before scrolling your John or Jane Hancock, be prepared to ask these questions.

✓ Will I need to supply my own furniture pads and mattress cartons?

✓ If I'm packing myself, what kind of containers are acceptable?

✓ Will the movers disassemble my furniture and reassemble it upon arrival and are there extra charges for this service?

✓ Following the initial cost calculation and weight estimate, will there be a reweigh to determine actual cost?

✓ Is there an extra charge for carrying items an excessive distance?

✓ Is there an extra charge for a stair carry or elevator carry?

✓ Is there an additional handling charge for moving my piano or organ?

✓ When is my estimated delivery window and how far in advance will the driver notify me that the truck is on its way?

✓ Upon arrival at my new home, will I need to pay the movers with cash or a money order?

✓ If I've purchased the company's liability insurance and I need to make a claim, what is the process?

 ## Make a Moving Memo

My questions for the movers:

_____

_____

_____

_____

_____

_____

Sure You're Insured?

To purchase or not to purchase…that indeed is the question! Think about it. You spent a lifetime working to accumulate everything you own, not to mention the irreplaceable heirlooms that you've picked up along the way, do you really want to throw caution to the wind of the open highway and risk losing it all?

We didn't think so!

Before you rest easy assuming that your homeowner's policy will cover your couches and credenzas en route, think again. Homeowner's policies rarely cover items in transit, and if they do, the fine print will most likely mention mileage limitations and interstate travel regulations. Even if that's not the case, the deductible on your policy might be too high to do you any real good. And, even if THAT'S not the case—you could be caught in a sticky situation if you're in the process of selling your home. Just when does that policy expire? Hopefully it won't be when Travis the Truck Driver pulls into the Exit 38 rest stop.

Are you getting the point that it's best to purchase insurance from your moving company

---

Tara's Tale—

Policy Schmolicy

We made the mistake of passing up the policy offered by our moving company. Instead, we banked on our homeowner's policy assuming we wouldn't need to use it. The minute we saw the movers catch the middle cushion of our soft leather couch on the stucco corner of our new entrance, we knew we were doomed. It wasn't worth forking out the $500 deductible to replace the $1,000 couch.

Even though we watched the movers watch us watch them damage our couch, they were in the clear because we hadn't signed their policy. Today, a lovely pillow hides their mistake and our bad decision.

Generally speaking, the major moving companies offer two liability options:

Full-Value Coverage

If you purchase this or a similar option from your moving company, you can expect to be protected for everything being moved up to the dollar amount that you declare when the contract is signed. If the driver loses, destroys or damages your items in transit, you can expect them to be repaired or replaced, or even receive a cash settlement for the market value of the items. Within the full-value coverage option, it is common to see tiered plans. With the higher priced policies you won't have any deductibles, but other, less expensive options will require you to pay deductibles if you file a claim.

Depreciation Coverage

If you choose a lump-sum value, pound weight value or room value, you can expect to be reimbursed based on the depreciated value of your missing or damaged items, up to the maximum value that you declare on your policy.

Because every moving company offers variations on the basic policies, we recommend sitting down with your moving agent and ironing out the details of your needs and coverage options. Whether you insure your household goods by weight, room or actual contents, just be sure to insure!

Insurance Inquiries

Before you sign on the dotted line, make sure you understand your fees and what will be covered in transit. Even after you read the fine print, ask your agent these questions:

- ✓ Are there any hidden deductibles or policy limitations?
- ✓ Will my antique dresser and Picasso be covered on this policy?
- ✓ If my computer or DVD player doesn't operate properly when I reassemble it, is it covered?
- ✓ If my stamp collection withers in the moving van, will I receive a cash settlement?
- ✓ How long after accepting my goods do I have to file a claim?
- ✓ Do I need to keep the damaged article in my possession for inspection?
- ✓ If I think a box or piece of furniture is missing, can I make a claim immediately?

Make a Moving Memo

Insurance questions for the movers and my moving company:

_____

_____

_____

_____

Do-It-Yourself

The least costly—and most adventurous—way to move is to rent a truck and do the packing, loading, driving and unloading yourself. The costs involved center around the size of the truck you'll need, as well as fuel, mileage rates and the price for pads, dollies and blanket rental. Keep receipts of your moving expenses because they might be tax deductible.

Driver beware. The risks involved with driving a larger truck should be carefully considered. An accident or even a highly stressful driving experience might not be worth the cost savings.

Shop Till You Drop

Congratulations! You've made the decision to rely on your own brawn work to get the job done. Before you whip out the bankbook, do a little brainwork to get the most bang for your buck. You might be thinking, "a truck is a truck" but we're sure you'll get a better bottom line after getting estimates from at least three rental companies. (And don't forget to check out *Section 4: Save Your Spine* for all the ins and outs of packing it up and moving it out!)

If you'll be making a one-way trip, it's best to start with the Yellow Pages and select national companies sure to have a drop-off location in your new city. Too many choices in the Yellow Pages? Rely on referrals from neighbors or coworkers who recently moved.

Before you start making the rounds to check out the movers, take the time to make a list of everything you'll be hauling to your new place so you can compare prices when the estimates roll in. And be sure to let the estimator in on everything you are moving, so you end up with the right size truck. After you get written estimates, compare the pros and cons of each and then make that reservation!

 ## Make a Moving Memo

Three truck rental companies and their estimates:

Company   Estimate

_____

_____

_____

_____

_____

Inquiring Minds Want To Know

What could be so hard about driving a rental truck? Don't wait until you fill up with unleaded instead of diesel to ask yourself, and the rental company, these questions:

- ✓ What is the truck rental fee?
- ✓ Are there additional mileage rates?
- ✓ Is there a charge for dropping the truck off in a different city?
- ✓ When I return the truck, should the gas tank be empty or full?
- ✓ Does the engine run on gasoline or diesel fuel?
- ✓ Is the transmission manual or automatic?
- ✓ Is the cab air-conditioned?
- ✓ How many seatbelts are in the cab?
- ✓ How does the lift gate operate?
- ✓ How many days do I have to return the truck?
- ✓ Do you offer roadside assistance?

✓ What are the additional fees for renting pads, dollies, blankets and wardrobe boxes?
✓ Are my household items insured during the move or do I have to purchase cargo insurance?
✓ Can I tow my car behind the truck?

 Make a Moving Memo

Additional questions for the truck rental company:

_____

_____

_____

_____

_____

_____

Ensuring You're Insured

Before you crank it into fifth gear, remember that most auto insurers won't cover you behind the wheel of a 25-foot moving van. Prior to packing your policy, check to see if you and your shiny rental truck are covered. If not, check with the rental company and discuss its optional protection plans.

Whether you and the value of your items are covered by the rental company or you have to purchase your own cargo insurance, consider the peace of mind you'll be buying when you climb into that truck and realize for the first time that, well, you'll finally be getting that lesson in driving a stick shift!

If you rent from one of the large national companies, you may be surprised that you won't exactly be going solo. Most national companies offer 24-hour emergency roadside assistance for those things that might go bump in the night. Whew!

Use More Than Your Eyes to Determine Size

It's time to talk trucks, where size really does matter. Before you rent a 25-foot van to move the contents of your studio apartment, do your homework. In the rental truck industry, it's common to find your options increase in size by increments of five feet. As a general rule of thumb, allow 150-cubic feet of truck space for each fully furnished room.

Misplaced your cubic foot measuring tape? We thought so! This handy guide will help you narrow your options.

A 10-foot truck will
> Move 1 or 2 rooms (a small apartment)
> Have approximately 390 cubic feet
> Withstand an approximate 3,200 pound load
> Have approximate interior dimensions of 10'x 6'4" x 6'

A 15-foot truck will
> Move 2-4 rooms (1 or 2 bedroom house or apartment)
> Have approximately 750 cubic feet
> Withstand an approximate 4,000 pound load
> Have approximate interior dimensions of 14'8" x 7'5" x 6'7"

A 20-foot truck will
> Move 4-6 rooms (a 3 or 4 bedroom house or apartment)
> Have approximately 1,200 cubic feet
> Withstand an approximate 7,000 pound load
> Have approximate interior dimensions of 21' x 7'10" x 7'4"

A 25-foot truck will
> Move 5-8 rooms (4 or 5 bedroom house)
> Have approximately 1,500 cubic feet
> Withstand an approximate 10,500 pound load
> Have approximate interior dimensions of 24'5" x 7'10" x 8'1"

Have Luck with Your Truck

✓ When shopping around and getting estimates, consider choosing a truck with a loading ramp similar to those used by the pros. You'll cut your loading time in half and save your spine in the process.

✓ Don't be fooled into booking a tall truck with more cubic feet than you need. It's the amount of floor space, not height, which makes the biggest difference.

✓ Most rental companies require the driver to be over the age of 18 and possess a valid driver's license—no need to stand in line at the DMV for that commercial license just yet!

A Place to Keep My Notes and Reminders…

Chapter 3

Meet and Greet Your New Community

"So, where ya goin'?"
"What are the job prospects?"
"How much does housing cost?"
"Is the weather better than here?"

Ah, the questions begin.

Whether you're moving a few blocks or several thousand miles away, it's a good idea to check out what you're getting into. And, if you're lucky, it will all be good: thriving economy, inexpensive housing, gorgeous weather…

If you're moving to a location not too far away from your present one, the road ahead of you is not only shorter, but easier. You can take a drive-by or two. Heck, you can get out and walk around! Start making friends with the neighbors and ask them:

- ✓ Where do the kids play?
- ✓ Where do teenagers hang out?
- ✓ Is it quiet during the day? At night?
- ✓ Is there a neighborhood watch? A Mrs. Kravitz?
- ✓ How about banks? Hardware stores?
- ✓ Where are the closest grocery stores, pizza places, donut shops, Greek cafés, taco stands? (Moving makes a person hungry!)

Also check out newspapers covering your new area and speak to local officials to see if there are any controversial plans being made, like the opening of a Buffalo Chip Bingo Hall.

Make a Moving Memo

Resources I'll gather from my new community:

____   Newspaper
____   Penny Saver
____   Telephone book
____   Real estate guides
____   Book of Lists

Other:

_____

_____

_____

A Little Further Away

Whether it's another city in the same state or a foreign place you have to practice pronouncing, no doubt the first place you'll turn to is www.HelpI'mMovingToANewPlaceThatIKnowNothingAbout.com. Okay, we made that site up. But you will be turning to everybody's informational friend: the Internet.

Many towns have Web sites of their own, for instance:

✓ Find a bite of the New York apple at NYC.gov
✓ Get up to date on everything in Kansas City, Mo. at KCMO.org
✓ Take a sip of Seattle at CityofSeattle.net
✓ Get a glimpse of the Golden Gate and monitor the fog in San Francisco at ci.sf.ca.us
✓ Before heading through the gateway in St. Louis make a stop at stlouis.missouri.org
✓ Blue skies and near-perfect temps await you in San Diego. See for yourself at sandiego.gov

✓ Planning to take a gamble on Las Vegas? Learn the odds at lasvegasnevada.gov
✓ Breeze by egov.cityofchicago.org to get wind of what's happening in Chicago.
✓ What time's tea in Boston? Set your watch according to cityofboston.gov
✓ Making Miami home? Make your first stop at ci.miami.fl.us
✓ If the southwest suits you best, visit Phoenix at ci.phoenix.az.us

Do a search for chambers of commerce, city newspapers, television stations, social clubs and real estate offices associated with your new community, and you'll probably end up with a great deal of information to help you out.

Chambers usually offer relocation guides with information on climate, living conditions, schools, economic conditions, etc. They are handy—but remember they usually paint a rose-colored picture. Also, if you're moving quite a distance, a couple of good resources for local weather conditions are *USA Today* or the Weather Channel—both give daily descriptions of weather around the country.

 Make a Moving Memo

Internet resources to surf:
weatherchannel.com
usatoday.com

_____

_____

_____

_____

_____

Of course, you can also spend an evening at the library and bookstore to do some research—and a little dreaming…

Donna's Ditty—

Friends in High Places

I was lucky because my good friend Daniel moved to San Diego first and was able to show me around the community. One of the best things he did was buy me a laminated map of the area. Back in Erie, I kept it by my computer so I could get an idea of the location of neighborhoods I was reading about on the Internet.

Get a hold of a phone book for your new community through the phone company covering your new area. Check out the services and places you may be frequenting including businesses, malls, grocery stores, police stations, churches—anything that will make you feel more at ease in your new "hometown."

If you have kids, call the schools your children will attend and talk to the guidance counselor or principal. Some questions to ask:

- ✓ How far is the school from my new neighborhood?
- ✓ Is it year-round or traditional?
- ✓ How do local math and reading scores rate?
- ✓ What are the sports programs like? The arts?
- ✓ What other types of programs are offered to suit my renaissance kid?

 Make a Moving Memo

Other questions to ask the school:

_____

_____

_____

_____

_____

For more information about moving your kids, go to Chapter 19: Don't Have a Cow, Dude! Children and Teens on the Move.

Donna's Ditty—

What Do You Mean There Are No MAC Machines?

Coming from "back east," both Tara and I get a kick out of the different terms we've found "out west," such as "ATM" instead of "MAC" machines. And there can be multiple personalities in the same state or even same city! San Diego is known as a conservative area of liberal California, although it does have its liberal pockets. The bottom line? No matter where you go, people are people—you'll find all kinds.

Cost of Living, Really Living

To find out how much day-to-day living will cost in your new locale, do a cost of living analysis. You can use online calculators or get one from your mover or employer. For a general picture, check the classified and store ads in your new community's newspaper to see how much it will cost to live there. Check out the cost of living calculator at bestplaces.net/html/cost_of_living.html as a starting point.

 Make a Moving Memo

Average Cost of:

Rent   _____

Utilities   _____

Cable   _____

Gasoline   _____

Groceries   _____

Insurance   _____

Gym   _____

Taxes   _____

Of course, if you can take a trip to your soon-to-be new home, that's even better! You'll be able to check things out in person and begin to learn the lay of the land.

Getting to know your new area will be valuable. It will help you feel more at ease during the first days in your new place when it seems like your whole life has been turned upside down. Remember to look at it as a new adventure—how many of us get a chance to start again with a clean slate?

A Place to Keep My Notes and Reminders…

SECTION TWO

Save Your Cents

This section of 29 Days to a Smooth Move *details how you can save money in packing and at tax time.*

Chapter 4:
Money Matters—Paying For the Packing Tape

For many of us, there's one question eating away at our brains—how much is this gonna cost?

Tissue, towels, twine, tape—it can add up! To give you an idea of just how much you'll be shelling out for the foam peanuts, we've put together some estimates of vital packing materials and other moving expenses and included a do-it-yourself moving budget so you can compute your costs down to the last Magic Marker.

Chapter 5:
Keeping In Touch With Uncle Sam

The flipside of practically buying stock in that Magic Marker company is that you can make some fine tax deductions. Most of the time.

Scraps of paper can become worth more than their weight in gold. Take a look at this chapter to discover how you can save money come April 15.

Chapter 4

Money Matters—Paying for the Packing Tape

Let's face it: moving does have its fair share of expenses, especially if your company isn't paying for relocation costs.

Both of us moved across the country paying our own way. Our advice to you is not to despair, there are ways to trim moving costs and move on a budget!

The Costs to Expect

The costs below were gathered from several moving supply company resources and office supply stores. No matter what your specific packing needs, this list will give you a good idea of what to stock up on—and what you'll have to shell out.

Packing Supplies

✓	3-ring binder (2")	$6.99
✓	Thick permanent black markers (3 of them)	$3.49
✓	Box with cell kit (for glassware)	$15.15
✓	Bubble wrap (box of 12" x 100')	$28.99
✓	Cat/small dog carrier	$49.99
✓	Clear sealing tape with dispenser	$5.99
✓	Contractor garbage bags (box of 32)	$11.87
✓	Dish pack box with cells	$15.15
✓	Electronics boxes	$9.95
✓	File storage boxes (6 pack of cardboard boxes)	$6.99
✓	Fire proof safe deposit box	$29.98
✓	Fragile labels (pack of 12)	$1.50
✓	Furniture pad (6 pack)	$135
✓	Heavy duty tape dispenser	$3.99

✓ Inkless newsprint (10 lbs.) $17.50
✓ Lampshade box $4.60
✓ Linen boxes $3.49
✓ Mattress bags (queen size) $6.50
✓ Packing peanuts (4 cubic feet) $14.99
✓ Picture/mirror boxes $6.99
✓ Room inventory labels (1 package) $8.65
✓ Towels and rags (use to pad boxes) $7.99
✓ Twine (1 roll) $1.58
✓ Utility knife or box cutters $8.99
✓ Wardrobe boxes (4 of them) $59.95
TOTAL   **$466.26**

Plane Tickets

If cross-country travel is in your plans, consider flying the friendly skies. While this may seem like a costly option, planning ahead can save precious pennies come boarding time. And, you'll get a free supply of nuts for your "Morning After Box" to boot!

✓ Average plane ticket cost per person   **$300**

Security Deposits

Ah, the ill-fated security deposit. For those of us who keep less than a "June Cleaver clean" apartment and who are headed for yet another apartment, the security deposit can be one sharp double-edged sword. Not only will you have to fork out some serious dough for the new management, you might be making a donation to your current landlord if your once white carpets are now beige.

✓ Average security deposit at your new apartment
(one month's rent)   **$700**

✓ Deposit lost from current apartment
(Gummy Bears couldn't be pulled from rug)   **$350**

Balance of Lease

Accept the simple fact that it's nearly impossible to time your move perfectly. Isn't it funny how leasing companies know this without you even telling them? Unless you're lucky enough to have a month-to-month lease, expect to lay cash on the line for the balance of your lease. We know what you're going to say: "But they can rent out my place after I leave, it won't take them five months!" Unfortunately, it's just the way it works.

✓ Average month's rent multiplied by months left on lease   **$700 (4)**

Movers/Truck

Chances are good that you won't know the exact cost of your move until every last muffin pan is loaded on the van and weighed. In most cases, your final bill will be based on the weight of your items and the distance the van will travel to your new home. Of course, don't be alarmed if your movers tack on extra charges for services performed by your agent, such as a stair-carry or piano move. In most cases, you'll be forewarned of extra charges.

It's extremely hard to calculate moving expenses because of the many variables involved. But this should give you an idea of what you'll be up against when it's time to put pen to paper in that checkbook.

Tara and her husband moved from Erie, Pa. to Las Vegas, Nev.—a total distance of 2,188 miles. Contents from their two-bedroom house weighed in at a hefty 4,440 pounds and did $3,705 worth of damage to their pocketbook.

Donna and her cats moved from Erie, Pa., to San Diego, Calif.—a total distance of 2,509 miles. Contents from her two-bedroom apartment (and what was left from her former four-bedroom house) tipped the scales at 4,982 (including a pick-up truck) and cost $4,036.

A greater distance and slightly more weight didn't seem to add that much more to the bill. Why the subtle difference?

It all came down to timing. Tara and Ron moved in July, one of the busiest moving months of the year. Donna relocated in January, one of the slowest months for moving. Frankly, Tara and Ron could have paid a lot more, but they carefully checked prices. And Donna may have found a mover that would have done it for less, however she decided to go with a recommendation from a trusted friend.

Cross-Country Trip

Planes and trains not tickling your fancy? Opt to go by automobile and you'll have more to consider than the price of gas. In addition to petrol, Happy Meals and sweet dreams at Motel 6, you'll need to budget for roadside emergencies and a little fun along the way!

Again, because the cost of a cross-country trip can vary widely, we'll provide you with Tara's log so you can get an idea of what you'll be munching and where you'll be dozing if you're on a budget. (Remember, these are 2001 prices and not adjusted for inflation!)

✓ Gas for a 2,188 mile road trip in a 2000 Honda Civic
(Filled up nine times) $92.23

✓ Four night's lodging (we're talking No-Tell-Motels here, not the Ritz Carlton) $177.47

✓ Food for two adults (My gosh! Did Tara and Ron do this on a shoestring or what? They typically ate two meals a day, one being tacos or McD's— but this also included splurges at Perkins.) $94

✓ Admission for two, please! There's no way Tara and Ron were driving across the country and not seeing the sweet land of liberty! Trip high-lights included stops at Graceland, Churchill Downs, the Grand Ole Opry, Oklahoma City Memorial and the Painted Desert. $38

For $401.70 you too can travel cross-country in a compact car, see every McDonald's along the way and even take in a little of "Heartbreak Hotel" if your schedule and wallet permit. Whatever you do, don't be in such a rush to get to your new city that you don't stop and smell the roses along the way. This is one great country, and you may never get the chance to see it from the open road again!

If you are traveling by car, it's a good idea to have about $300 extra cash on hand to handle those unforeseen circumstances, like flats and overheated radiators. If you prefer credit to cash, make sure you know your credit limit and consider increasing it for safety's sake before you hit the road.

Rental Car

If you choose to fly to your new home, you will most likely arrive long before the stork delivers your Subaru. Make arrangements ahead of time to pick up a rental car at your destination airport.

- ✓ Average cost of a compact car (Chevy Cavalier) for one week. This includes surcharges and taxes. Rates may be higher or lower based on city, availability and season. (You'll find cheaper rates at non-airport sites.)
  $150

Closing Costs of Selling a Home

Because this topic is so complicated and will vary widely, we recommend you seek the advice of a lending or mortgage professional. While it's safe to say that these fees will vary widely, you can no doubt count on dropping a chunk of change into closing costs.

Costs Upon Arrival

Don't put away your purse just yet! You'll need to consider the costs of getting settled in your new town. Budget for these incidentals ahead of time and you won't be as shocked when the credit card bill arrives.

- ✓ Grocery shopping (Don't skimp on restocking your cupboards—you need to regain your strength!) **$200**

- ✓ Toiletries etc. (You're bound to find a Wal-Mart where you can supply yourself with tissue, cleaning supplies, personal and miscellaneous household items.) **$150**

- ✓ Vehicle registration (This will vary widely by state.) **$200**

- ✓ Application fees for drivers' licenses (Again, this will be different for each state.) **$50**

- ✓ Long distance phone calls (Don't worry—you're allowed to be homesick!) **$100**

Since what used to be a local call will now cost more than a quarter, a new location is a good excuse to check out what alternative long distance plans are available to save you money! Of course, you'll also need to budget funds for re-establishing all of your utilities and services, like cable and Internet service. And, if you're about to begin a job hunt, don't forget to set aside a few hundred dollars for that spiffy new suit that's sure to land you the position. (Psst, need direction in how to organize your job hunt? We have a manual for that, too! Check out *Get A Job! Put Your Degree To Work* on page 231 and at GetAJobBook.com.)

	29 Days to a Smooth Move Budgeting Worksheet		
I Need It	**Description**	**Estimate $**	**Actual $**
	MOVERS		
☐	Professional movers		
☐	Truck rental		
☐	Gas for rental		
☐	Additional mileage expenses		
☐	Hand truck/dolly		
☐	Furniture pads		
☐	OTHER:		
	PACKING SUPPLIES		
☐	3-ring binder		
☐	Black markers		
☐	Boxes with cell kits		
☐	Bubble wrap		
☐	Cat (or dog) carrier		
☐	Clear sealing tape and dispenser		
☐	Dish pack boxes		
☐	Electronics boxes		
☐	File storage boxes		
☐	Fireproof safe deposit box		
☐	Fragile labels		
☐	Furniture pads		
☐	Inkless newsprint		
☐	Lampshade boxes		
☐	Linen boxes		
☐	Mattress bags		
☐	Packing peanuts		
☐	Picture/mirror boxes		
☐	Room inventory labels		
☐	Twine		
☐	Utility knife		
☐	Wardrobe boxes		
☐	OTHER:		

	CLEANING SUPPLIES		
☐	Dumpster rental		
☐	Carpet cleaning service		
☐	Cleanser		
☐	Contractor garbage bags		
☐	Sponges/Scouring pads		
☐	Towels and rags		
☐	Professional cleaning service		
☐	OTHER:		

	MOVING OUT		
☐	Balance of rent on apartment		
☐	Lost security deposits on apartment		
☐	Home repair/selling preparation costs		
☐	Home closing costs		
☐	Balance of mortgage		
☐	OTHER:		

	GETTING THERE		
☐	Plane tickets		
☐	Auto inspection		
☐	Rental car		
☐	Gas for road trip		
☐	Lodging en route		
☐	Food		
☐	Entertainment		
☐	Auto Emergency Fund		
☐	OTHER:		

	SETTLING IN		
☐	Rental car		
☐	Grocery shopping		
☐	Household items		
☐	Toiletries		
☐	Vehicle registration		
☐	Driver's license application fee		
☐	New suit for job hunting		
☐	Security deposit		
☐	First month's rent		
☐	Deposit on home		
☐	OTHER:		

	SETTING UP UTILITIES/SERVICES		
☐	Cable/Satellite service		
☐	Cell phone service		
☐	Electric		

☐	Fuel/Gas		
☐	Gym membership		
☐	Internet service provider		
☐	Newspaper subscriptions		
☐	Sewer/Trash/Refuse		
☐	Telephone service		
☐	Water		
☐	OTHER:		

Description	Estimate $	Actual $
MY MISCELLANEOUS ITEMS		

**GRAND TOTAL		

A Place to Keep My Notes and Reminders…

Chapter 5

Keeping in Touch with Uncle Sam

It's the Tax Man

Stop the shredder! Before your moving receipts hit the circular file, consider that many of your expenses qualify as deductions on your federal income tax return if you are moving because of a new job.

Do you qualify to deduct moving expenses on your tax return? Take these two simple tests and find out:

The 50-mile distance test:

Your new primary workplace must be at least 50 miles farther from your old home than your old workplace was from your old home. Confused? So were we. Don't think about it, just use this worksheet to see if you qualify for the distance test:

Miles from your old home to your new workplace	1. ___ miles
Miles from your old home to your old workplace	2. ___ miles
Subtract line 2 from line 1. If zero or less, enter -0-	3. ___ miles

Is line 3 at least 50 miles?
__ Yes. You meet this test. Go on to the Time Test.
__ No. You do not meet this test and cannot deduct your moving expenses.

Time Test

If you passed the distance test, you're halfway there. Here's the other half of Uncle Sam's catch—you must also work full time in the city where your new job is located at least 39 weeks within the year after the job location change.

Confused again? We thought so again!

It's not so bad really because you don't need to be working for the same employer during those 39 weeks and the 39 weeks don't need to be consecutive. So you can take those two weeks off to visit your mother-in-law after all.

Keep in mind that the time you spend looking for work doesn't figure into those 39 weeks. And, either you or your spouse can qualify, but don't get crafty and assume that you can add your total hours clocked together. Unfortunately, the loopholes aren't that big.

If you're self-employed, the stakes are even higher. You must work at least 78 weeks full-time in your new city within 24 months after the change. And keep in mind that at least 39 of those work weeks must be within the 12-month window after you change residences.

Luckily, you don't get extra points for understanding the rules. You just have to pass the tests!

The source for these tests is Department of the Treasury Internal Revenue Service, Publication 521, Moving Expenses. Check it out online at irs.gov to read the nitty gritty—there's loads more fine print where this came from—we just hit the highlights.

Why so many rules? It's the darn students and craft-fair-goers that ruin it for the rest of us. These guidelines usually stop professional students and hobbyists who string beads a few hours a week from getting a tax break.

If you passed both the distance and time tests, congratulations! Chances are your direct moving costs are tax deductible, but check with your tax advisor to be sure.

Donna's Ditty—

When In Doubt...

Ask! Even after doing some of the math, I didn't think I would be eligible for deducting my moving expenses. When I mentioned it to my accountant, though, she gave a resounding "Sure, you can!" I happily took the tax breaks.

Tax Deductible Moving Expenses

Now that the hazings are over and you're officially in Uncle Sam's Fraternity, start deducting! Keep receipts for every aspect of your move in a large envelope. Worry about categorizing once you're settled in your new home. The following items are generally tax deductible:

- ✓ Any part of the purchase price of your new home
- ✓ Car tags and driver's license
- ✓ Expenses of buying or selling a home
- ✓ Expenses of getting or breaking a lease
- ✓ Home improvements to help you see your home
- ✓ Loss on the sale of your home
- ✓ Losses from disposing of club memberships
- ✓ Meal expenses
- ✓ Mortgage penalties
- ✓ Pre-move househunting expenses
- ✓ Real estate taxes
- ✓ Refitting of carpets and draperies
- ✓ Security deposits (including any given up due to the move)
- ✓ Storage charges except those incurred in transit and for foreign moves
- ✓ Temporary living expenses

 Make a Moving Memo

The Items I Can Deduct:

_____

_____

_____

_____

_____

_____

Non-Tax Deductible Moving Expenses

While the tax code can be very beneficial to those who qualify, don't get carried away.

Tara's Tale—

Love Me Tender, Taxman!

Come tax season, we were surprised to hear our accountant chuckle after we handed over our moving receipts, which included admission for two to Graceland. Slightly embarrassing lesson learned: entertainment en route to your new home is not tax deductible.

The following items typically cannot be deducted as moving expenses on your federal tax return:

- ✓ General car repairs, maintenance, insurance or depreciation of your car
- ✓ Pre-move house-hunting expenses
- ✓ Temporary living expenses
- ✓ Meals
- ✓ Expenses associated with buying or selling a home
- ✓ Home improvements to ready a home for sale
- ✓ Loss on a home sale
- ✓ Real estate tax
- ✓ Driver's license and storage charges except those paid in-transit
- ✓ Entertainment during the road trip to your new city

Use Form 3903 to figure your moving expense deduction and deduct your moving expenses on Form 1040 (consult your tax professional for the specific line number as it may vary by year). IRS tax publications can also be ordered by calling your friendly neighborhood IRS agent at 1-800-829-3676. And, be sure to consult a tax professional for the deductibility of your specific moving expenses. While the lists we've provided serve as a general guideline, it's best to rely on a licensed professional to help with your specific tax situation. For more information on deductible and nondeductible expenses and reimbursements, visit irs.gov.

(Source for this chapter: Department of the Treasury Internal Revenue Service, Publication 521, Cat. No. 15040E, Moving Expenses, for use in preparing 2004 returns)

A Place to Keep My Notes and Reminders...

SECTION THREE

Save Your Securities

This section of 29 Days to a Smooth Move *details how you can make the most when selling your home, save the most when leaving your apartment and have peace of mind knowing that everyone from the babysitter to the beautician has been told of your move.*

Chapter 6:
Prepping Your Lily Pad For Sale
Not only do you have to pack everything underneath the roof, you have to sell the roof, too!

Selling your home presents its own unique challenges—what will you fix up and what will wait to challenge the new owners? When should you put it on the market? How can you make it a must-see for potential buyers? Wouldn't it be easier to jack up the place and move it slowly down the road like you see on TV?

We have the answers to your questions! (Except for that last one—you're on your own if you choose to literally move your house!)

Chapter 7:
Apartment, Sweet Apartment
Not so fast! Leaving an apartment is certainly easier than selling a house, yet before departing your rental unit you have some details to take care of so you get as much of your security deposit back as possible.

Here are some tips for getting your rented space looking and smelling sweet.

Chapter 8:
Attention! Attention! I Am Leaving the Premises!
The list making continues. You have to tell today's version of the butcher, the baker and the candlestick maker that you will no longer be needing their services. And don't forget to inform the aunt who always kisses you on the lips that you may be seeing her a little less often.

Chapter 9
On the Prowl for a New Place?
Ready to go but don't know where you're going? Life can be that way sometimes. Here's some help in reading the classifieds when you're looking for a roomie—or a house of your own!

Chapter 6

Prepping Your Lily Pad for Sale

Turn, Turn, Turn...

To everything there is a season, and the real estate market is no exception.

While your moving timeline might not perfectly align with these guidelines, it's good to be aware of the ebbs and flows in the home buying market so you at least know what to expect when it comes to listing your home.

Home sales are worst in January, with only 5.6 percent of all closings happening during the blustery month. And, it's no surprise that August is the busiest month in the industry; 10.4 percent of all closings end up on August's books—just in time for the kids to enroll in school. As the temperatures rise, so do home closing percentages. The stats for May, June and July come in a close second only to August.

 Make a Date

Important Date! The house is going on the market:

_____

_____

Make a Moving Memo

My asking price is:

_____

_____

Before you wait until Mother's Day weekend to pound your "For Sale" sign on the front nine, remember that it will take an average of three months from the time you receive a contract until you hand over the keys. Before listing, consider the number of homes on the market in your neighborhood and—above all else—*when* you need to move!

Make a Moving Memo

Other homes for sale in my neighborhood:

Address   Listed Price

_____

_____

_____

_____

_____

_____

Bing. Bang. Boom.

Strap on your tool belt, grab a hammer in one hand and a toilet bowl brush in the other—it's time to get busy! We know, we know, you've only got 29 days to move. But, if you're selling your home, the extra time you spend now will pay off big come closing day.

Make a Moving Memo

Must-do house projects before the sign goes up:

Room/Location   Task

_____

_____

_____

_____

_____

_____

_____

_____

_____

_____

Don't forget the patio, deck and garage!

It's no secret that many folks buy homes because of the emotional appeal. When it comes time to house hunt, look beyond the bright yellow wall that you've always wanted. Instead, ask yourself if the floor plan suits your needs. Were you dead set against a two-story home and now you're caving?

While some let their emotions get the better of them, others have hard-core practical reasons for choosing a pad in a new place. Some families relocate to be in the school district of their choice. Others want low- or no-maintenance yards. There are those that get giddy at the thought of a guard gate. Still others want a home office with an separate entrance. Just remember, there are no right reasons for the home you want—only your reasons. Make a list of pros and cons before you sign on the dotted line and be sure you really *have* found the house of your dreams.

Tara's Tale—

It's True What They Say...

First impressions are everything. Be tidy, not spotless—after all, your house is a home, not a showroom. Don't make the mistake of taking on a major renovation project that could put you in the poor house and delay your listing date.

Follow these steps to make a great first impression!

The Front Yard

✓ Paint the front door. Go with burgundy, deep olive, blue or gray in super high gloss. Create the illusion of opulence by installing that brass lion head knocker with the ring in its mouth—we know you always wanted one!

✓ Make a stop at the superstore's garden center and fix up a large terra cotta pot of geraniums for the front porch.

✓ By all means, mow the lawn.

✓ Even if you haven't cleaned the windows in the fifteen years you've lived in your house, now's the time to either get out the Windex or call in the pros. Crisp is key.

✓ Replace rusty gutters instead of painting them. Do the same with that dilapidated mailbox.

Tara's Tale—

Picking and Passing Projects

Just where did Ron and I draw the line when it came to pre-sale home improvements? Despite our desire to paint the exterior trim on our brick home a new shade of green, we opted to suffer through the pea soupiness of the original color and concentrated our efforts on the inside. It paid off—we had several interested bidders in the first week alone.

The Inside

- ✓ Bathrooms should be spotless. Make your toilets sing about your cleaning abilities and leave no sign of mildew in the shower.
- ✓ Replace bathroom carpets. Remnants are cheap and the freshness will invite potential buyers in.
- ✓ De-clutter. Remove the Doritos bags from the top of your refrigerator, recycle the newspapers under your coffee table and deep six your collection of bath-gels-of-the month from your vanity. Organize under sinks and in closets too.
- ✓ Clean or replace your carpets and floors. There is no bigger turn off than filth and stains. Before you bring in Bob Vila, consider buffing and waxing wood floors yourself. Hire a professional carpet cleaning service to tackle the beige rugs, and, if that doesn't work, consider replacing them.
- ✓ Just like mowing the lawn is a must for the outside, the same goes for making beds on the inside.
- ✓ Only arrange flowers where they would normally be expected. Don't turn your pad into a funeral parlor.
- ✓ Do you have a fireplace? Pile in the logs and pinecones for an oh-so-homey feeling.
- ✓ Replace soiled switch plates with shiny white ones.
- ✓ Clean the chandeliers and light fixtures and ditch the dead bulbs for glowing ones.
- ✓ And yes, potential buyers should be able to eat off the kitchen floor.
- ✓ Tile grout got you grumpy? These days there are "bleach pens" that can take it away!
- ✓ "De-personalize" your house by doing away with family photos. Prospects will have an easier time picturing themselves in the space without visual reminders of your wedding, your baby shower and your trip to Bermuda.
- ✓ Peee-ewww! Your house can look fantastic, but if it smells less than lemon-fresh, you'll be jeopardizing your sale. Consider boarding dogs and cats a few weeks prior to inspection to lose odors and if you smoke, take it outside. Learn the laws of fresh bread, cinnamon and coffee and you'll be well on your way to signing on the dotted line.

    Fresh bread: Splurge on a loaf of Italian bread, break open its belly, lather it with butter or vanilla and pop it in the oven at medium heat about two hours before the inspection begins. Don't blow it—remove the bread before the folks arrive to inspect your oven!

Cinnamon: You don't need to turn your kitchen into a Cinnabon to achieve the aroma. Just warm a few tablespoons in water in a pan in the oven and let it work magic.

Coffee: It's the equivalent of a homebuyer's aphrodisiac. A coffee cup of beans roasted in your oven will do the trick. Add some jazz in the background and you just may have enough to purchase a top-of-the-line espresso maker for yourself!

The Backyard

- ✓ Is your patio furniture looking good? Get rid of the milk crates you use as backup seating.
- ✓ If you have a tool shed, make sure the paint isn't peeling.
- ✓ The pool must be perfect. No matter the season, keep it leaf and scum free.
- ✓ Make sure the pooch's poo is out of sight…and smell!

No matter how much prep work you do, keep in mind that the potential buyer has been out scouring neighborhoods for weeks, looking at home, after home, after home. The devil is in the details—try to put your best foot forward at all times.

Preshowing Checklist

You've done all the basic cleaning, but before you have that open house, take a run through your place and look for (or hide):

- ✓ Dirty dishes
- ✓ Soap scum in the sink
- ✓ Less than lovely toilets
- ✓ Paw prints on the kitchen floor
- ✓ Damp towels
- ✓ Dust in sunny places
- ✓ Odd smells

Make a Moving Memo

List your own home's peculiarities (such as a faucet that has to be shut off extra hard not to drip). Take care of the items on this list before a showing since they are things you don't want to spot just as potential buyers are coming up the walk:

_____

_____

_____

_____

_____

_____

Tara's Tale—

What Were They Thinking?

When we were househunting in Las Vegas, we passed up a model just like the one we ended up buying because of the wall-to-wall pink carpet. Even if the sellers would have knocked money off the asking price, we weren't up for the headaches and hassles of replacing the cotton candy. Question some of your own decorating decisions—if they stand out like a sore thumb, it may be time to rip out, paint or otherwise change before putting the house up!

Set the Stage for a Quick Sale

Really want to make your house appealing to prospects? Consider hiring someone to "stage" your home. Home stagers are professionally trained to make a house look its best to buyers.

Proponents say any home can be staged to look better and sell more quickly. (Sometimes for a price several thousand more than you originally dreamed of!)

Typical changes made by someone staging a home include trimming back plants, adding a fresh coat of paint and even bringing in new furniture.

If you're interested about getting your home staged, ask your real estate professional about it or do some Internet research on your own. It just may be your ticket to a fast sale at a great price!

What If the Fish Aren't Biting?

You can probably think of a hundred reasons why your house isn't selling. But really, it all comes down to two things:

1. The price isn't right for current market conditions.
2. The condition of your home isn't where it should be for the price you're asking.

Before you throw in the towel, cancel your flight reservations and start unpacking boxes, consider your options:

✓ Give your place a facelift. Although Tara's husband Ron always says "you can't dress up a pig," there are some surefire ways to give your space some pizzazz without breaking (or breaking into) the bank. If you didn't repaint, now's the time to get rolling. While you may love your 24-foot purple walls, Barney is unlikely to buy your home. These distractions may be a real turn-off to potential buyers. Get fresh by going neutral.

✓ Get a new listing number. If your home has been on the market for a few months, the MLS (multiple listing service) number will look old and many agents only search new listings. Take your home off the market for a few weeks while you repaint and then relist.

✓ Slash your price. If your home is already in tip-top shape and you haven't had so much as an offer, it may be time for a blue light special. Don't prostitute your property, just lower the sale price enough to make it more attractive to potential buyers. What are similar-sized homes in your neighborhood selling for? Undercut those prices and you'll be on your way to an offer.

✓ Change agents. If your agent hasn't called in two weeks or doesn't remember your name when you meet, it might be time to go shopping for a new broker. Ask your friends and neighbors for referrals. Often times, agents specialize in specific neighborhoods.

✓ Help out a first-time buyer. While you want to benefit from the sale of your home as much as the buyer, don't let something small be a deal breaker. Throw in the kitchen appliances to sweeten the pot. You can also make a deal on closing costs, real estate taxes or offer a home warranty.

Tara's Tale—

Warming Up the Buyer

After living through three frigid winters in our uninsulated brick house in Erie, we sold it only to learn of the potential deal-breaker after arriving in Nevada. Before closing, we had to replace the 62 year-old pre-WWII boiler/heater/monster in the basement so the new owner would be toasty warm and not die of carbon monoxide poisoning. After shelling out $3,000, we bought her a shiny new heater. We hated to do it but were willing to get her to sign on the dotted line.

One small consolation is that Ron and I now wear shorts in February, while she'll run her new toy until May when the snow melts in Erie.

A Place to Keep My Notes and Reminders...

Chapter 7

Apartment, Sweet Apartment

If you're moving out of a rented home or apartment, you have special items to consider.

First, locate your lease and review its terms about giving notice. Do you have to give 30 days' notice from the first day of the month? Will you have to pay out the balance of your lease? When (and if) will you receive your security deposit back? Are you responsible for having the spaghetti sauce stains cleaned from the carpets before you vacate?

Going Down

Even though you might be feeling stress right now, consider Mr. Roper's feelings too—where in the world will he find a tenant as good as you?

After the tears are dried, be sure to schedule the freight elevator for your moving day. And, it won't hurt to ask the building manager if the interior walls of the elevator could be padded the morning of your move.

Donna's Ditty—

"Lobby, Please!"

I thought I had it all together when moving from my Erie apartment to San Diego—except I forgot to schedule the freight elevator on moving day! My movers arrived at 9 and someone else had dibs on the elevator at 10. Even with me practically nipping at their heels, the movers couldn't get everything out in under an hour. Luckily, the others had a fast move, too, and we were able to finish up after lunch!

Read over your lease and ask your building manager what needs to be done. Some of the tasks most likely include:

✓ Giving your building manager notice and scheduling moving-related needs. Arrange parking space for the truck at both the pick-up and delivery addresses.

✓ Schedule a time to have an apartment walk through with the manager, who will want to make sure you're leaving it in the same condition as when you arrived.

✓ If you're leaving an apartment or home you rent, review your lease and determine what will need to be cleaned and polished. Usually it's things such as carpets, ovens, refrigerators and windows. (If you're really ambitious, you'll fill in the picture holes on the walls with toothpaste.)

✓ It's not as complicated as selling a home, but you still have to worry about disconnecting cable and phone service so you won't get charged when you're not there. Check with your building manager to see if electricity and gas shutoffs are in order, too.

✓ Allow time to clean and do last-minute touch ups after the movers are finished. The moving of boxes and furniture can undo much of the cleaning you did. Don't be in such a hurry to follow your furniture out the door that you leave the apartment in less-than-security-deposit-return condition.

Donna's Ditty—

How Much Is Your Time Worth?

It's important to be meticulous, but there is a place to draw the line when it comes to spending time and money. For instance, I had some apple pie juice baked to the bottom of my apartment's oven and spent three hours of valuable "last week before I go" time (plus $45 in not-so-easy-off cleaners) trying to get it off. I didn't succeed, and it took the building manager all of two seconds to look at it and say, "That'll be $25 off your deposit."

Make a Moving Memo

Leaving the apartment to-do list:

☐ Apartment manager notified of moving day.
Day _____ Time _____

☐ Elevator/moving van parking space scheduled.

☐ Walk through with manager set.
Day _____ Time _____

Other stuff to shiny up or schedule before leaving my digs:

_____

_____

_____

_____

_____

_____

A Place to Keep My Notes and Reminders…

Chapter 8

Attention! Attention! I Am Leaving the Premises!

Dear Mr. Postman

Changing your address with the post office couldn't be easier now that there's a quick secure online form at moversguide.usps.com. (When we moved, we actually had to *drive* to the post office and complete the form with an old-fashioned pen—can you imagine?)

At the site, simply select the date for the post office to begin forwarding your mail to your new address, complete the change of address form online, verify your information and click submit.

Deliver this letter—de sooner de better! Publishing companies like at least four weeks' notice and early notification can avoid postage-due costs from other senders.

The U.S. Postal Service does charge a $1 fee for this service and asks you to submit your credit card before your address change will be accepted. Don't balk at the buck! The procedure helps prevent fraud. The U.S. Postal Service verifies your identity with a valid credit card—money well spent.

If you insist on doing it the old-fashioned way, Mover's Guides are also available at your local post office or from your postal carrier.

Tips for Completing the Change of Address Form
- ✓ If only you are moving, select the "individual" option on the form.
- ✓ If your entire family has the same last name and is moving to the new address, select the "family" option. If *anyone* with the same last name is *staying* at the old address, select the "*individual*" option. In all cases,

family members with *different* last names or those family members moving to *different* addresses must prepare *separate* forms.

How Long Will My Mail Be Forwarded and What Will It Cost?

Gone are the days of the Pony Express! You'd never guess the complexity of categories and classifications used by the U.S. Postal Service. We went right to the source for an accurate breakdown.

- ✓ **First-Class Mail, Priority Mail and Express Mail** are forwarded free of charge for one year.
- ✓ **Newspapers and magazines** are forwarded free of charge for 60 days.
- ✓ **Standard Mail** (formerly Standard Mail A) is not forwarded unless the mailer requests it. This category includes circulars, books, catalogs and advertisements weighing less than 16 ounces.
- ✓ **Package Services** (formerly Standard Mail B) is forwarded locally, free of charge for one year. Moving outside the local area? Be prepared to pay additional forwarding charges. This category includes packages weighing 16 ounces or more not mailed as Priority Mail.
- ✓ **Special Services** like Certified, Collect on Delivery (COD), Delivery Confirmation, insured, registered, Signature Confirmation or special handling mail is forwarded without additional fees when mail is being forwarded to a domestic address only. Mail is subject to the applicable postage for each specific service.

Still have questions? Call a friendly U.S. Postal Service customer service representative at 1-800-ASK-USPS (1-800-275-8777).

Utilities to Cancel

Whether you're a homeowner or a renter, you'll need to contact your utility companies before moving on. Plan ahead with this worksheet, so the next occupant's water bill doesn't spill into your lap.

Make a Moving Memo

Utility	Phone #	Call Date	Confirmation #
Gas			
Fuel			
Electric			
Water			
Sewer			
Trash/Refuse			
Telephone			
Cell Phone			
Answering Service			
Cable			
Satellite TV			
Internet Service Provider			
Cable Modem Provider			
OTHER			
OTHER			
OTHER			

You're not done yet! Never thought you knew so many people, did you? Now it's time to start notifying government offices, your service providers, the banks and don't forget...Aunt Clara!

Office	Phone #	Call Date	Confirmation #
Veterans Admin.			
Library			
City Hall			
Tax Assessor			
DMV			
Social Sec. Admin.			
State/Fed. Income Tax Bureaus			
OTHER			
OTHER			
OTHER			

Change of address Notify the IRS of your new address with form 8822, *Change of Address.* You'll find an address for your nearest IRS service center on the back of the form.

Service Provider	Phone #	Call Date	Confirmation #
Accountant			
Beautician			
Chiropractor			
Dentist			
Doctor #1			
Doctor #2			
Doctor #3			
Doctor #4			
Financial Planner			
Handyman			
Insurance Agents			
Lawn Service			
Lawyer			
Manicurist			
Masseuse			
Pool Service			
Real Estate Agent			
Snow Service			
Stock Broker			
Water Softener Service			
OTHER			
OTHER			

Office	Phone #	Call Date	Confirmation #
AAA			
Agencies you donate to (United Way, Red Cross)			
Auto Service Station			
Banks			
Book/CD Clubs			
Credit Cards			
Credit Union			
Dry Cleaner			
Fine Dining Clubs			
Fitness Club			
Florists			
Lien Holders			
Mortgage Company			
Pharmacy			
Places You Volunteer			
Schools/Colleges			
Video Stores			
Wine & Cheese Clubs			
OTHER			
OTHER			
OTHER			

Publication	Phone #	Call Date	Confirmation #
Alumni Newsletters			
Church Bulletin			
Fashion Catalogs			
Magazines			
Newspapers			
Trade Publications			
OTHER			
OTHER			
OTHER			

Don't Forget Family and Friends!

While notifying your Book of the Month Club of your new address is certainly a priority, don't forget to let Aunt Clara in on your new contact information too. Go through your address book and prepare a list of friends, coworkers and relatives who should be notified of your move.

Planning to say goodbye in person? Distribute contact cards with your new information. You can slip these into back pockets when its time for that tearful hug goodbye. Contact cards are available at office supply and greeting card stores. They're cute, perforated and ready for your printer.

There are many online options now for creating your own change-of-address cards. You can print and mail them yourself or have an online vendor do all the work for you with a few clicks of a button. Visit your favorite search engine and type in "change of address cards" for the lowdown. Yes, it doesn't smack of the personal touch, but it does reek of convenience!

Utilities to Connect at Your New Residence

Whaddaya know! This list looks similar to the one to you completed before you left your old place. Well, it's back, and you need it again if you don't want to finish this book by candlelight.

Utility	Phone #	Call Date	Confirmation #
Gas			
Fuel			
Electric			
Water			
Sewer			
Trash/Refuse			
Telephone			
Cell Phone			
Answering Service			
Cable			
Satellite TV			
Internet Service Provider			
Cable Modem Provider			
OTHER			
OTHER			
OTHER			

A Place to Keep My Notes and Reminders…

Chapter 9

On the Prowl for a Roomie—or a New Place?

Decoding the Classifieds

Roman tub, vaulted ceilings, stainless steel appliances *and* crown molding? Congratulations on locating the apartment of your dreams! You might be exhausted from weighing the pros and cons of an upstairs versus downstairs versus corner unit, but there's more to consider.

Will your spare bedroom be reserved for your Rottweiler or a roommate? If you're wincing at memories of dorm days gone bad, stop for just a moment. Maybe a roomie wouldn't be so dreadful. After all, a spare bedroom buddy would provide built-in companionship, someone to share the expenses with and maybe…just maybe…it's a friendship waiting to be made. And the best part? You'll actually have a kitchen this time around (no hot pot necessary!).

No Others Need Apply

Sounding good? Okay—now all you need is the perfect roommate! Before you start cruising the produce aisle for bait, hop online and check out your new community's newspaper. Most newspapers post the classifieds on their websites. Whether you're ISO of a N/S PF or an SWM whose DDF, you might just find it in the want ads.

Don't worry. It will make sense in just a minute.

SWF ISO N/S MBA PM

Are you a single white female in search of a non-smoking married but available professional male? We thought so! (Hey, we just explain the codes, what you do with your roomie is your business.) Unlike ZIP code and area code finders, handy references for decoding the classifieds are harder to come by. What acronyms do you fancy?

BiF = Bisexual Female
BiM = Bisexual Male
BIMF = Bisexual Married Female
BIMM = Bisexual Married Male
CD = Cross-dresser
CPL = Couple
DBF = Divorced Black Female
DBM = Divorced Black Male
DDF = Drug and Disease Free
DWF = Divorced White Female
DWM = Divorced White Male
GBF = Gay Black Female
GBM = Gay Black Male
GWF = Gay White Female
GWM = Gay White Male
ISO = In Search Of
MBA Married But Available
MBF = Married Black Female
MBM = Married Black Male
MJF = Married Jewish Female
MJM = Married Jewish Male
MM = Married Man
MWC = Married With Children
MWF = Married White Female
MWM = Married White Male
N/S = Non-Smoker
PF = Professional Female
PM = Professional Male
SAF = Single Asian Female
SAF = Single Asian Male
SBF = Single Black Female
SBM = Single Black Male

SCM = Single Christian Female
SCM = Single Christian Male
SHF = Single Hispanic Female
SHM = Single Hispanic Male
SINK = Single Income No Kids
SJF = Single Jewish Female
SJM = Single Jewish Male
SOH = Sense of Humor
SPARK = Single Parent Raising Kids
SWF = Single White Female
SWM = Single White Male
TG = Transgender
TS = Transsexual
TV = Transvestite

Home Sweet Bigger Home

What?! You found three of the world's best roommates and need to swap the dream apartment for more square footage? Turns out, roommate seekers aren't the only ones who speak in code. Realtors can be your best resource for finding a home or apartment in your new community…if you speak their language.

Brush up on the jargon before clearing out the free home finders on the newspaper stand.

Real Estate Pro Speak

3B/2B	three bedrooms, two bathrooms
assum. fin.	assumable financing
dk	deck
gar	garage
gard	garden
fab pentrm	fabulous pentroom (sometimes with a view)
FDR	formal dining room
frplc, FP	fireplace
grmet kit	gourmet kitchen
HDW, HWF	hardwood floors

hi ceils	high ceilings
nr bst schls	near the best schools
pvt	private
pwdr rm	powder room, or half-bath
upr	upper floor
vw, vu, vws	view

And, for understanding what you'll be getting in your "necessary room"...

full bathroom	includes toilet, sink and bathtub
¾ bathroom	includes a toilet, sink and shower
½ bathroom	includes a toilet and a sink
powder room	another term for a ½ bath

There you have it—some of the ins and outs of finding a new place to live. TTFN!

A Place to Keep My Notes and Reminders…

SECTION FOUR

Save Your Spine

This section of 29 Days to a Smooth Move *gets down and dirty on the specifics of packing and your physical move.*

Chapter 10:
Sort It Out Before You Pack It Up
The problem with moving is that most of us have made mountains out of our homes, as in peaks of possessions and hills of hodgepodge. Read on to get motivated in releasing your grip on what weighs you—and your moving van—down.

Chapter 11:
Packing No-No's
There are some items that you just can't safely pack—or simply aren't allowed to transport. Peruse this chapter to get the low down about what must be left behind.

Chapter 12:
Packing (and Carrying) Yes-Yes's
Where did my moving manual go? There are some things that just shouldn't be put in a box and covered with clear tape. Before you mistakenly seal up your box of packing supplies, look over this information for ideas of what should stay in your sight and by your side.

Chapter 13:
Have Yourself a Pack Attack
Does packing have you panicked? Or is this what you've been itching to do all along: box up the stuff and stack it in the corner? It's some of the most gratifying moving work you'll do. Discover our top tips to get packed in tip-top shape!

Chapter 14:
There's Got to Be a Morning After Box
Hon, where's the coffee? It's 6 a.m. the day after your move. Bushed and bleary-eyed, make sure you have the essentials to make your first day in your new home a happy one.

Chapter 15:
The Dawn of Moving Day
It's finally here! Are you ready? (Everybody give a resounding "Yes!") Get a good start to your moving day by following these helpful hints, and we'll make sure you get there in one piece!

Chapter 16:
Welcome Home: Moving-In Day on the Receiving End
The fun doesn't end once you wave bye-bye to your former community because, unfortunately, you can't live out of the moving van! Our words of wisdom ensure your washer ends up where it belongs.

Chapter 10

Sort It Out Before You Pack It Up

Does packing have you panicked?

Before you even begin to think about using that shiny new tape dispenser, you need to get organized, get garbage bags and get sorting.

Start in the easiest room. For Tara it was the kitchen because that was the most organized, and she could do it fast for a sense of accomplishment. Donna started with shelf after shelf of books she knew she'd have no time to read in the next few months anyway. It doesn't matter where you think your best starting point is— the point is to get started! Then work your way through the house making progress one room at a time.

Make piles of items that don't belong to you and don't be afraid to put those contractor garbage bags to the test with items that you know can't be sold, donated or recycled.

Return and Retrieve

If you're like most of us, you'll have trunk loads of everything from beanbag chairs to Weed Whackers to return to your parents, neighbors and friends. Before you drive to the other side of town to return a serving spoon, make a plan. Who have you borrowed from most?

Write each person's name on a large box and fill it with his or her belongings. Continue to fill the boxes and start new ones until you're done with the last room.

In between rooms, take a break and make a list of everything you're missing. Have you lent out kitchenware, sporting equipment, books and tools? Organize your list by "lendee" and give those people a call to let them know that you're moving and that you'd like to take your casserole dish with you!

Schedule all of your drop-offs and pick-ups for one or two evenings and be sure to thank your lenders. Use this opportunity to bid farewell to those you won't see again before you move.

 Make a Moving Memo

I have to return stuff to:

Person   Item

_____

_____

_____

_____

_____

_____

Make a Moving Memo

I have to collect my stuff from:

Person   Item

_____

_____

_____

_____

_____

Seek and Clean

Don't underestimate the amount of time it will take you to clean out your current abode, and we're talking the darkest corners of your damp basement and the crawl spaces that haven't seen a human since you tossed your high school yearbooks up there 20 years ago.

Just like sorting, go room by room to avoid feeling overwhelmed. Clean well now and reap the rewards when you unpack!

 Make a Moving Memo

Cleaning supplies I need to get the job done:

_____

_____

_____

_____

_____

_____

Donna's Ditty—

Look Out Beloooooooooowwwww!

One of the most exhilarating days of my life is when I had a dumpster delivered to my home on the farm. Since most of the stuff I was throwing away was on the top floor, I filled garbage bag after garbage bag, sealed them all tight and pitched them out the window to the waiting dumpster. Long before "live simply" became a credo of the generation, I got started by getting rid of what was not needed. It felt great and made my moving day tons easier on myself and the backs of my friends!

I Want It All, And I Want It Now

Now is the time to start thinking practically. It might be difficult, but simply resign yourself to the fact that you can't keep everything. A little judgment during clean out will go a long way when it's time to load the moving van and write a check to the movers.

Don't forget, if you're leaving your move to the pros, your final bill will be based on the weight of your boxes. Can you part with your dusty collection of *Good Housekeeping* magazines? Dismantling and moving your satellite dish might cost more than buying new upon arrival. Why not leave garbage cans, sink strainers and laundry baskets behind and plan a trip to the dollar store in your new community?

Also, set aside those valuable items you want to carry with you.

 Make a Moving Memo

My most precious possessions that should not board the van:

_____

_____

_____

_____

_____

_____

_____

_____

_____

_____

_____

Donna's Ditty—

Let Your Fingers Do the Walking

What was the most important item I schlepped from Erie to San Diego? The Erie area phonebook! Whether you use it to order flowers for a sick aunt or need to get in touch with an acquaintance who somehow didn't make it in your address book, you'll find the "old phonebook" worth its weight in gold. Do not pitch it!

Along the way, you'll run across items that have value to them, but just not to you anymore. Set them aside and…

Hold a Garage Sale in 10 Easy Steps

Would you like to convert that growing pile of hodgepodge into a pocketful of cash? Use this guide to hold a garage sale in 10 easy steps!

1. **Pick your co-hosts.**

   Invite friends, relatives and neighbors to join in. More sellers, less work. More items, more buyers. Start saving your plastic grocery bags now for your shoppers. (Have each member at a group sale mark his or her items with a different colored dot—no mix ups!)

2. **Pick a date.**

   The early bird really does get the worm when it comes to garage saling. Weekends work best with morning and early afternoon hours. And, it won't hurt to select a "rain date" from the get-go. (Be prepared. Some pros will show up an hour early to get a jump on the treasure hunt!)

3. **Pick a location.**

   If you're too far off the beaten path to attract traffic, consider asking a friend or relative to set up shop in their yard. (In exchange, offer to sell some of their used items alongside yours.)

4. **Do your homework.**

   Check the bylaws where you will hold your sale. Do you need a permit? Do you need to get the neighbors' permission? (Plan ahead and avoid over-the-fence disputes!)

5. **Advertise.**

   Hang flyers on grocery store and post office bulletin boards. Post an online notice on your community Web site. If you have a front gate, tie a bunch of helium balloons to it on sale day to direct traffic your way. (Advertise "cash only" on your fliers and the day of your sale, if that's your policy, and attract buyers by listing hot items.)

6. **Get cash and coins.**

   Make a bank run the Thursday before your sale (banks are busiest on Fridays). Decide if you will deal with checks, hold items, have a dressing room or deliver large items. And don't forget the calculator! (Note your initial "cash count" so you can celebrate the day's profits when the garage door slams shut.)

7. **Setup the night before.**

   Organize similar items together on horizontal surfaces (crates, card tables and plywood on sawhorses work great). Hang clothes on a clothesline. (Don't mix items for sale with those not for sale, like your son's bike, or your son, in the garage.)

8. **Price smart.**

   Instead of sticking price tags to each item, make category signs: "All video games $5." Start pricing at about 1/5 of the item's original cost and adjust depending on condition. (Don't waste time on nickels and dimes. Price everything to the nearest dollar or quarter.)

9. **Be cautious.**

   Yard sales are prime targets for shoplifters. Keep valuable items close to your station or position a friend or relative to watch the area during the sale. (Instead of a cash box, how about a fanny pack for cash and coins?)

10. **Slash prices!**

    Announce a blue light special about two hours before your sale ends. You don't want to take the items with you! (Donate leftover items to charity and make sure you get a receipt for tax purposes.)

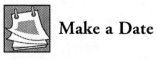

Make a Date

To-do lists for having a garage sale:

Date and time: _____

Location: _____

Rain date: _____

Make a Moving Memo

Friends and family I'll ask to join in:

Person   **Response**

_____

_____

_____

_____

_____

_____

My sale's "Hot Items" to promote:

_____

_____

_____

_____

_____

_____

People I can borrow tables from:

_____

_____

_____

_____

_____

_____

Advertising

☐   Fliers posted in grocery store (week before sale)
☐   Classified ad placed (to appear a few days before sale)
☐   Signs hung (day before sale)

Materials for "Check Out"

☐   Change box (or fanny pack)
☐   Change
☐   Calculator
☐   Bags
☐   Paper
☐   Pen

Other:

_____

_____

_____

_____

_____

_____

Remember to have fun at your garage sale! Don't let wheeler-dealers frustrate you. It's part of the game! Have a pan of brownies and a pitcher of iced tea near the cash station for those working the sale. Pass the time away and entertain sellers with your favorite tunes and before you know it, you'll be heading back to the bank to make a deposit!

 Make a Moving Memo

Household items to donate:

_____

_____

_____

_____

_____

_____

_____

_____

Donna's Ditty—

Sold! To the Smiling Man in the Back!

When my parents passed away, my dad left my sister and me at least one of every tool—and two of most! Instead of trying to sell those and a bunch of farm equipment we knew nothing about, Teresa and I had an auction. I highly recommend it if you're not exactly sure of the worth of your many household items. We ended the day with a tidy sum—and an empty garage!

Tara's Tale—

What's the Cost of Four More Wheels?

If you're moving cross country and have two cars, seriously consider selling one of them—it'll save you a ton in shipping costs! We decided to drive the newer of our two Hondas to Vegas and sell its red older brother. Before calling the classifieds and pounding signs to oak trees, we put out feelers to family and friends. Lo and behold, Ron's Uncle Gary was interested! With all of the changes happening in our lives at once, it was comforting to know that our Honda would be under the care of a relative.

A Place To Keep My Notes and Reminders...

Chapter 11

Packing No-No's

As tempting as it might be to sneak spray paint, conceal candles and tuck turpentine into the dark corners of your moving boxes, don't do it.

All of your possessions will be loaded into a moving van where temps can rise to well over 150 degrees. By law, movers may not accept hazardous materials for shipment.

And even if you're moving yourself, packing combustibles could ignite disaster. Leave these items aside before you start packing.

Restricted items include:

- ✓ Aerosol cans
- ✓ Ammonia
- ✓ Ammunition and firearms
- ✓ Batteries (including auto batteries)
- ✓ Bleach
- ✓ Candles
- ✓ Charcoal
- ✓ Chemistry sets
- ✓ Cleaning fluid
- ✓ Fertilizer
- ✓ Fireworks
- ✓ Frozen food
- ✓ Industrial chemicals
- ✓ Kerosene
- ✓ Lacquer remover

- ✓ Lighters
- ✓ Lighter fluid
- ✓ Loaded weapons
- ✓ Matches
- ✓ Muriatic acid
- ✓ Nail polish remover
- ✓ Motor oils and fuels (gasoline, diesel, aviation fuel)
- ✓ Oxygen
- ✓ Paint
- ✓ Pesticides
- ✓ Plants
- ✓ Pool chemicals
- ✓ Produce
- ✓ Propane
- ✓ Spray paint
- ✓ Spray starch
- ✓ Sterno cans
- ✓ Tar remover
- ✓ Turpentine
- ✓ Varnishes
- ✓ Weed killer

Donna's Ditty—

Halt, Who Goes There?

California is very protective of its agricultural industry. I had to sign a waiver with my moving company stating I would not be including foliage of any kind in my shipment—and I made sure to comply. Lucky for Tara (see below) Nevada doesn't have such stringent rules!

Tara's Tale—

I Must Confess a Slight Insanity Defense!

Although we had gifted away more than 40 houseplants, I just couldn't part with my "mosquito bite healing" aloe plant. Like a puppy dog, it sat at my feet for more than 2,000 miles as we made our way across the country in the middle of the summer heat. That plant spent many a night on Motel 6 nightstands and actually lived to tell about it! (Hint: It's okay to be a little irrational considering what you're going through.)

A Place to Keep My Notes and Reminders…

Chapter 12

Packing (and Carrying) Yes-Yes's

The following items present no safety hazards but can create hassles and headaches if your shipment is delayed or worse…lost. Carry irreplaceable and sentimental items with you or make arrangements with your banker for their transfer.

- ✓ Address books
- ✓ Airline tickets
- ✓ Bonds
- ✓ Car keys
- ✓ Checkbooks
- ✓ Coins
- ✓ Computer software and discs
- ✓ Deeds
- ✓ Files
- ✓ Furs
- ✓ Financial statements
- ✓ Home videos
- ✓ Insurance papers
- ✓ IRAs
- ✓ Jewelry
- ✓ List of online usernames and passwords
- ✓ Medicine
- ✓ Original artwork
- ✓ Photos
- ✓ Research projects
- ✓ School records

✓ Stamp collections
✓ Sterling silver
✓ Stocks
✓ Tax records
✓ Wedding albums

 Make a Moving Memo

Items not to let out of my sight:

_____

_____

_____

_____

_____

_____

A Place to Keep My Notes and Reminders...

Chapter 13

Have Yourself a Pack Attack

Don't Panic

WARNING: You are about to be overwhelmed. Breathe deep. Without a doubt, packing is the most daunting part of the moving process, but you will survive AND succeed! With the help of this moving manual, family, friends and a little positive thinking, your boxes will be signed, sealed and ready to be delivered according to schedule. Get a glass of wine and c'mon—let's get moving!

Packing Supplies Checklist

Whether you're moving out of an efficiency apartment or an estate with servant quarters, collect these essentials before you get packing. And remember, what seems like "a little" will end up "a lot" once you start the process of stacking and stuffing. Don't underestimate how much you really do own!

- ✓ Expandable file for receipts and other paperwork
- ✓ 3 thick permanent black markers
- ✓ Boxes with cell kits (for glassware)
- ✓ Bubble wrap
- ✓ Cat carrier
- ✓ Clear sealing tape with dispenser (Buy at least 5 rolls to start—you won't believe how fast this goes!)
- ✓ Contractor garbage bags (These bags are near-impossible to rip.)
- ✓ Dish pack boxes with cells
- ✓ Electronics boxes
- ✓ File storage boxes (Never leave your full file cabinet to the movers. More on this in "Tara's Tale" below.)
- ✓ Fire proof safe deposit box
- ✓ "Fragile" labels

- ✓ Furniture pads
- ✓ Heavy duty tape dispenser
- ✓ Inkless newsprint
- ✓ Lampshade box
- ✓ Linen boxes
- ✓ Mattress bags
- ✓ Packing peanuts
- ✓ Picture/mirror boxes
- ✓ Room inventory labels
- ✓ Tissue paper (Dollar stores have it for cheap!)
- ✓ Towels and rags (Use these to pad boxes in lieu of bubble wrap)
- ✓ Twine
- ✓ Utility knife or box cutters
- ✓ Wardrobe boxes

Tara's Tale—

A Less Than Sticky Situation

If you think three rolls of packing tape will get the job done, time to unroll your expectations! In the wee hours of the morning on moving day, I was dialing the local U-Haul to see what time it opened. I ended up going back not once, but twice, to accommodate last minute sealing needs. And, stick with clear tape. The brown variety will give you nothing but the blues.

Tips From The Pros

Before You Begin

- ✓ Collect at least 25 more boxes than you think you will need.
- ✓ Separate boxes by size and place appropriate size boxes in each room before you begin.
- ✓ Line up supplies next to your boxes when packing—don't accidentally pack away your scissors!
- ✓ Reinforce the bottom of each box with a strip of packing tape going in each direction.

General Rules of Thumb

✓ Keep the weight of boxes reasonable, trying not to exceed 35 pounds.

✓ Pack one room at a time.

✓ Label each box with a brief description of its contents and room destination.

✓ No bulging or sagging boxes please! Avoid collapsed and ruptured boxes by filling in spaces.

✓ Heavy items on bottoms of boxes, lighter items on top.

✓ Use "Fragile" labels on boxes with breakables to alert movers to handle with care.

Special Hints For Special Items

✓ Stack books in small boxes, laying them flat and alternating bindings to prevent warping.

✓ Use larger boxes for linens, towels and clothes.

✓ Use paperback books to pad the sides of boxes with empty corners and spaces.

✓ Pack CDs vertically in boxes instead of stacking them flat.

✓ Prevent breakage by wrapping lids separately. (Don't want a broken cookie jar!)

✓ Avoid messes by sealing opened jars and boxes before packing them and putting them in plastic bags in case of spillage. (Really though, you can buy a new jar of jelly upon arrival.)

✓ Use an extra large box for lampshades and cushion them with soft pillows.

✓ Load area rugs last so they can hit the floor before your furniture does at the new place.

✓ Fill your washer/dryer with clothes, linens and other light or awkward items.

✓ Bundle cords and tape them to the back of lamps and appliances.

✓ Use rope to secure furniture doors and drawers, tape will damage wood.

✓ Pack dishes upright in double-wall corrugated dish boxes with cell packs (dividers).

✓ Check the owners' manual of large appliances for special moving instructions and how to secure doors.

✓ Move clothing on hangers in wardrobe boxes, garment bags or sturdy garbage bags posing as garment bags (use twine to secure all hanger necks together).

✓ Pack electronics in original boxes or wrap pieces in plastic bags and pack in heavy-duty boxes.

✓ Tape an "X" of masking tape over the glass part of mirrors and pictures before wrapping them in bubble wrap. It will keep the wrap from smudging the glass.

✓ Protect those mirrors and pictures further by securing corrugated cardboard corners over them.

✓ Wrap exposed furniture legs in bubble wrap or newsprint, wrap in furniture pads and tie securely.

✓ Keep things sanitary by using the correct size mattress pad to protect your bed.

 ## Make a Moving Memo

The hardest items I have to pack, and how I plan to do it:

_____

_____

_____

_____

_____

_____

_____

_____

_____

_____

_____

Tara's Tale—

Stick By Me, Kid, I'm Going Places!

If you disassemble any furniture, make sure to put its nuts, bolts, screws and hardware in a plastic bag and tape the bag to the item itself. We forgot this crucial step and Ron's corner computer desk sat on the floor in three parts until the manufacturer received our sob-story letter and was sympathetic enough to send us replacement hardware.

Tara's Tale—

Avoid a Soiling

While wrapping fragile items in newspaper might seem like a great way to save money, remember that newsprint ink never thoroughly dries. Unless you want to rewash all of your crystal goblets when you unpack, purchase inkless packing paper at an office store.

Pack in Stages

One of the easiest ways to get your house (and your mind) organized is to pack in stages.

Start with the items that you don't use everyday, like seasonal decorations, items in storage and that china that's just collecting dust.

It won't even look like you made a dent when you're done with phase one. Don't worry! Things will look bare in a hurry when you move on to knick-knacks, books and home accessories. Last but not least, bare the walls and clear your closets and cupboards.

Allow plenty of time to:

✓ Break down computers and pack them properly
✓ Empty your fish tank (Tara and Ron made the mistake of doing this an hour before the movers arrived!)
✓ Love your lampshades (A little extra care when packing lampshades goes a long way and will save you a bundle from having to replace them.)

Donna's Ditty—

The "I Don't Know" Pile

One night I was packing like a woman possessed and I came across a wicker basket that just stopped me cold. Keep or throw away. I could not decide. That's when I started my "I Don't Know" pile. When it took longer than five seconds to decide, the item went there. After a day or two, I revisited the pile and it was much more clear about what had to come with me!

Tara's Tale—

Computer. Hello, Computer!

As an extra precaution, we backed up all of our computer files on CD and left a copy at my mother-in-law's house in Erie for safekeeping. (Since the brain gets fuzzy at this stage, make a note that the idea is to do this before you power down your computer system.)

When the rubber of the moving van hits the road, there's a slim chance that your hard drive could bite the dust if it's not properly packed. Plus, don't make the mistake of tossing the backup CDs into the computer carton because that defeats the purpose!

Inventory of Boxes: The Organized Organizer's Important Step!

Want to know where things are, where they're going and where to find them when you get there? Create an inventory of boxes.

As Tara was packing, she kept a tablet with her and jotted down every item that disappeared into a box. After sealing each box, she assigned it a number, wrote it on the side and top of the box and next to its contents on her notepad. She also scrawled its destination room in big black letters on the box and again, on her tablet. When she was completely done, she typed all of the info into her computer and made a master list.

When the movers arrived at her new residence, all she had to do was sit back with her trusty list and strike numbers as each box entered the front door.

Tara's Tale—

Her Most Valuable Item

With my self-created inventory list, I had total peace of mind knowing that everything we packed was somewhere in our new apartment—not in a dark corner of the truck. And, during the unpacking phase, I just referred to my list to find out where things were hiding.

Now, you're probably thinking that this is way over the top—but you can achieve the same results by following these simple steps:

- ✓ Keep your moving manual by your side while you're packing.
- ✓ Start with #1, write a brief description of the first box's contents in your manual and draw a big black #1 on that box.
- ✓ Based on the contents decide the destination room. Write it on the box and your list.
- ✓ Seal it and move on to #2, continuing the same process until the last box is sealed.
- ✓ Congratulations! You have a complete inventory of boxes. Make a copy for your fireproof box (for insurance purposes).
- ✓ On moving day have your inventory handy and cross off the numbered boxes until the truck is empty!

Donna's Ditty—

Um, well, hmmmmm…

Don't tell Tara, but I didn't do an inventory of boxes. While I totally agreed with it in theory, I just didn't have the time. The most organized I got was labeling my boxes "bedroom" or "bathroom" and relying on the little yellow stickies from the moving company to keep count of my possessions. While a self-made inventory is the best way to go, it's not the end of the world if time constraints won't allow it.

F-R-A-G-I-L-E

Aw NUTS! Before you blow your entire moving budget on foam peanuts, visit your favorite grocery stores, appliance stores, gift shops and craft stores. You'll be surprised how much good packing material you'll get free for the asking.

- ✓ Cut big Styrofoam sheets from appliance stores to fit your boxes and use as an inner padding for breakables.
- ✓ Use cartons of adequate size and strength.
- ✓ Tape all like hollow items together (cereal bowls, mugs, etc.).
- ✓ Wrap all fragile items individually in newspaper, magazine pages or bubble wrap.
- ✓ Use linens, rugs, towels, curtains and pillows to pack fragiles.
- ✓ Paper cushioning between layers and on the exterior sides of boxes absorbs shock. Don't skimp on the newsprint.
- ✓ Burn the bulge and make sure your cartons aren't busting at the seams.
- ✓ Use twine to avoid in-transit carton bursts.
- ✓ This is not the time to conserve space! Look how those glasses were shoved in your cupboard—don't decide to give them breathing room now. Loosely packed items are more likely to be damaged. Use plenty of padding to ensure dishes and other breakables can't move in the box.
- ✓ Last but not least, write F-R-A-G-I-L-E in huge letters on your box.

Tara's Tale—

I'll Drink To That!

There's more in store than alcohol at your local liquor store. When it came time to pack books, I called employees of the closest State Store (as we used to call them in Pennsylvania) to ask if I could take some boxes off their hands. Not only did they supply more than 20 durable cartons with nifty dividers, they let me pull up to the back door and personally loaded my trunk for me! (What a friendly lot liquor store employees are!)

Donna's Ditty—

Covering All Sides

After congratulating myself for packing some things well ahead of time, I soon began cursing my enthusiasm when I had to dig through dozens boxes to find an item I needed NOW.

Packing and repacking got tiring, so I began labeling the top and all four sides of the box with its final destination, such as "Bathroom—Toiletries." Visible from all sides, I knew where to start in the stack when I had to dive back in for something important.

Special Needs Packing

Can't find a box big enough to fit your canoe?

If you'll be moving large items such as hot tubs, large screen TVs, treadmills, boats or pool tables, you may need the help of a third party service to assist with special needs packing and shipping.

The same holds true for pre- and post-move servicing of appliances, grandfather clocks, kayak pools and satellite dishes. Since the rules on this topic vary, it's best to consult your mover about the special services they offer for moving large items.

Make a Moving Memo

Items needing special consideration:

_____

_____

_____

_____

_____

_____

Tara's Tale—

Filing Cabinet: The Aftermath

When we talked about emptying out our file cabinet and keeping the documents under our watchful eye during the move, it didn't seem like a priority.

But when the movers arrived in Las Vegas and delivered a kicked-in cabinet with busted locks, our choice to leave it packed quickly topped the list of the dumbest things we'd ever done. So, moving-in day turned into calling-and-canceling-every-credit-card-and-bank-account-we-had-ever-opened day.

Take a memo: make sure no credit card numbers or other important identification numbers are accessible in your stuff!

Dealing with Flammables

By now, you know that moving combustibles is a no-no. But, keep in mind that moving tanks, trimmers and tools filled with the stuff is also prohibited.

- ✓ Empty oil and gasoline from your lawn mower, Weed Whacker, edger, chainsaw and snow thrower.
- ✓ Discard or donate cans of paint, cleaners and other flammable products.
- ✓ Visit your local propane gas dealer to have your refillable tank for your grill emptied and sealed properly. Toss all non-refillable tanks.

A Place to Keep My Notes and Reminders...

Chapter 14

There's Got to Be a Morning After Box

Necessary Box...Morning After Box...I Need It Now Kit...

No matter what you call it, label it "OPEN ME FIRST" and make sure to load it on the truck last or to keep it by your side so you'll have it at your fingertips when you arrive at your new residence.

Use this list to determine what makes sense for you. And, if you're moving a family, have members pack their own survival kits.

What's Necessary for The Necessary Box?

Cleaning Supplies

- ✓ Cleanser
- ✓ Scouring pads
- ✓ Sponge/Rags
- ✓ Trash bags

Kitchen

- ✓ Aluminum foil
- ✓ Coffeemaker and filters (or directions to the nearest Starbucks!)
- ✓ Dish soap
- ✓ Disposable cups
- ✓ Paper plates
- ✓ Paper towels
- ✓ Pet foods/bowl
- ✓ Plastic utensils
- ✓ Saucepan

Snacks

- ✓ Bag of apples
- ✓ Bottled water
- ✓ Breakfast bars
- ✓ Coffee
- ✓ Pringles
- ✓ Ramen noodle soup
- ✓ Phone number to the nearest pizza shop!

Tools

- ✓ Flashlight
- ✓ Hammer
- ✓ Light bulbs
- ✓ Nails
- ✓ Screwdrivers (straight and Phillips head)
- ✓ Tape measure
- ✓ Utility knife

Bathroom

- ✓ Bar soap
- ✓ Hair dryer
- ✓ One towel per person
- ✓ Shampoo
- ✓ Shower curtain and rings
- ✓ Toilet paper
- ✓ Toothpaste and toothbrush

Everything Else

- ✓ Change of clothes
- ✓ Extension cord
- ✓ Favorite toys for the kids
- ✓ First aid kit
- ✓ Important documents (medical, insurance, inventory of boxes)
- ✓ Phone

- ✓ Pillows
- ✓ Sheets—one set per bed
- ✓ Valuable jewelry
- ✓ Your address book

Tara's Tale—

Snug as a Bug

If you're moving long distance, there's a good chance that you'll arrive before your belongings. Instead of sheets, we had a sleeping bag and pillows in our Necessary Box. That kept us happy campers until our bed arrived a week later!

A Place to Keep My Notes and Reminders…

Chapter 15

The Dawn of Moving Day

It's time!

Moving day has arrived—if you've been following along, there should just be a few quick things to take care of before you head out to your new locale.

 Make a Date

My moving day is:

_____

Considering Your Worst Nightmare

You might have some lingering fears, such as:

- ✓ Your loading volunteers don't show up.
- ✓ Your moving truck doesn't appear.
- ✓ Your rental truck won't start.
- ✓ Your babysitter bails.
- ✓ Someone gets hurt from hurrying.
- ✓ The weather is not cooperating.

The best way to prevent such moving day catastrophes is to plan ahead. You've been using your moving manual—it can help you here as well!

Some ideas to help you avoid the bothers above:

- ✓ Call your mover the day before to confirm arrival time.
- ✓ Inspect your moving rental vehicle on pick-up and make sure it's been serviced (get a special inspection on the tires).
- ✓ Touch base with your helpers and babysitter and confirm the day, time and location they'll be needed.
- ✓ Make sure everyone is alert to avoid accidents.
- ✓ The weather, well, we can't help you with that. But keeping a sunny disposition goes a long way!

Donna's Ditty—

Neither Rain, Nor Sleet, Nor Unplowed Roads...

The dawn of the day I left Erie found me, and my cat Baby, peering out a hotel window—and looking at 14 inches of snow blanketing the parking lot (and still falling)! Grrrrr! As if this whole thing wasn't stressful enough!

I can still feel the relief and happiness wash through me as I spotted Tara and her trusty Honda Civic plowing through the white stuff to safely deliver my kitty and me to the airport—you definitely can get by (and get out!) with a little help from your friends!

What Should Be Done

At the dawn of moving day, all your boxes should be packed (unless your mover will be doing it) and just about everything should be ready to carry out of the house and onto the truck.

Start your day the right way and:

- ✓ Have everyone boost their energy levels by eating a good breakfast. (Pay a last visit to a favorite local restaurant and you won't have to clean up!)
- ✓ Strip the sheets off all the beds.
- ✓ Get the young kids and pets out of the way at a babysitter or kennel (whichever makes more sense).

✓ Put older children to work sweeping up rooms, carrying the lighter boxes, making room labels for the doors of the new house (Home Office, Brandon's Room, etc.) or other duties that will keep them productive and part of the process.

✓ If you hired movers, prepare a sketch of your new place and label or number the rooms to coincide with the way your boxes are marked.

Make sure you separate the items you will be taking with you so they don't end up on the truck! And don't forget to leave your "Morning After" box out for last on, first off or to take in the car with you.

 Make a Moving Memo

Moving day jobs and who gets to do what:

Job   Person

_____

_____

_____

_____

_____

_____

_____

The Lowdown On Loading

If you're moving yourself, here are some tips on conducting the physical labor—without having to plan a stop at the emergency room!

✓ Plan ahead for parking space. Do you need a permit? Does Ned the Neighbor need to move his Nissan?

✓ Park as close to the entrance of your house as possible and use a spotter, not your X-ray vision, to back up safely.

✓ Learn the lessons of the lift gates from the rental company before trying it on your own.

✓ Make sure the loading ramp is sitting securely on a flat surface.

✓ Be generous with blankets! Most rental trucks are not "air-ride" and you'll want to protect your furniture with blankets and plastic sheeting.

✓ Appliances on first, followed by furniture (bend at the knees, not at the hips!).

✓ When it comes to boxes, stack lighter ones on top of heavy. Slightly angle the boxes toward the front of the truck to compensate for in-transit movement.

✓ Fill "holes" with boxes and soft items, slide long items along the sides.

✓ Couches and tables go great against the truck walls, but be sure to tie them down.

✓ Prop pictures and mirrors on edge, or tuck them between larger boxes.

✓ Keep your eye on the load lines marked on the interior walls.

✓ Finish off your load with a square item, like your box spring or ping pong table, to create a flat wall where the bulkhead will fall.

✓ Lock 'em up, latch 'em tight and ship 'em out!

When Do I Get to Sit Down?

Gee, doesn't a person get a break? Well, you kind of do at this point—if you hired movers, that is!

Once you greet the movers at the door and take care of any business with them, the important thing is to stay accessible—but also stay out of the way. It's time to let them do their job, with your most strenuous activity jotting down the box numbers going by for your personal inventory.

Take advantage of the opportunity and put your feet up for a few minutes before they take the chair you're sitting in out from under you!

Pass the Key

It is time to leave the home that has given you so many memories. It's good karma to leave your home in a clean condition for the new owners. Also, spiffying it up will help you see if there is anything that you may have forgotten.

Pay particular attention to the closets, cabinets and drawers. Leave any instructions to the appliances and mechanical systems. Take one more walk through for your final inspection.

Donna's Ditty—

Who You Gonna Call?

To make it easier on my former home's new owner, I left a list with the names and phone numbers of all the service personnel who were familiar with the place's furnace, plumbing and lawn mowing needs.

Your Mover's Top 10 Wish List

Who can say it better than the pros? After working with and talking to several moving companies, we've come up with a list of what the movers want from the "movees" for a perfect day.

1. Be prepared. Read moving booklets, ask questions, get a written estimate and reserve your mover well in advance.
2. Really be prepared. Pack up loose items. Have your share of the work done. Tear down your appliances, computers and stereos for moving.
3. Be equipped. Separate your traveling items, clothes and still-needed household essentials.
4. Be lean. Trash, donate or sell stuff you no longer love or need.
5. Be available. The movers will have questions.
6. Be good to yourself and your family. Remember the importance of enough sleep and food for energy. Stress and hurrying can cause problems.
7. Be smart. If packing yourself, use protective padding and paper. It's worth the investment.
8. Be organized. Label boxes, cupboards or rooms before your moving day to help get your items to the right rooms at delivery.
9. Be aware. Young children and pets should be out of the way and supervised.
10. Be calm. By using your to-do lists and keeping a sense of adventure, you and your family will move happy!

A Place to Keep My Notes and Reminders...

Chapter 16

Welcome Home! Moving-In Day on the Receiving End

If You're a Do-It-Yourselfer

If you trucked cross-country or even cross-state with your brood and belongings in tow, there will be loads to do when you arrive at your new home.

Unlike your moving counterparts who paid drivers to haul their heaps and had days to ready their empty spaces before the drivers arrived, you'll be compressing this activity into one or two days. But don't fret—this manual will get you there.

If You Feed Them, They Will Come

Whether you rely on the brawn of your firstborn Biff or the brains of Billy the Boy Scout, be sure to feed them plenty.

Unlike professional movers, who typically don't accept meals, your family, friends and recent hires will expect everything from bagels to pizza and pizza bagels. It's a small price to pay for the helping hands, so don't skip this step.

If you start before noon, designate a kitchen counter for bagels, cream cheese, OJ and water. Make a mid-afternoon break appealing by bringing in subs or pizzas and, of course, a few cans of cold beer stocked in the fridge wouldn't be a bad touch either (for the adults, not the Boy Scouts).

Keep it simple with paper plates, cups and a nearby trash bag for easy clean-up. Helpers expect a little bit of chaos, but a few refreshments will go a long way to letting them know that you appreciate them and their backs.

Make a Moving Memo

Food Items For Moving Day:

Item   Phone number (order in!)

_____

_____

_____

_____

_____

_____

Tara's Tale—

The Toast of the Town

On the morning of our move, we relied on the neighborhood bakery for the usual fare—bagels, cream cheese and muffins.

Because some people like their bagels toasted, we decided to load the toaster oven on the truck last so our friends could enjoy their morning treat golden brown. You would have thought we gave them 24-carat gold jewelry!

This little step went a long way to letting them know how much we truly appreciated their help on an early Saturday morning. (But don't think you have to treat professional movers with kid gloves—they don't expect you to serve them vittles before they get going.)

If You Hired Movers…

There's no better advice we can offer than to simply leave it to the pros.

When they come to your door to haul away your stuff, most of your work is done. To make the day easy on everyone, make sure kids and pets are out of the way and things that aren't going on the truck are in one area and labeled that they're staying put.

And If You Didn't...

Don't despair! You no doubt have some friends and neighbors lined up to help you move. The more people you can convince that this will be fun, the easier (and more fun) it will be.

It helps if you have everything boxed up and ready to go when your help arrives. Keep a First Aid Kit nearby for unexpected mishaps, along with plenty of refreshments for break time!

If one of your crew members has especially good "spacial qualities," station him or her in the moving truck to organize the boxes and bags as they come in. Refer to our packing tips in Chapter 2 and Chapter 15 so the back of the moving truck stays organized all the way to your new destination.

After everything's packed up and en route, take a few moments to go through your "old" place to make sure you have everything. Then it's time to hit the road yourself—and start life in a new place.

Moving with Movers

Unless your move is less than a day's drive away, it's likely different people will be delivering your good than took them away. On the day your stuff arrives, start out on a positive note. If you haven't been keeping the carpet warm, make sure you arrive at your new residence an hour or so before the movers. Not only will a late arrival on your part set a bad tone for the events to follow, there could be a waiting charge if you are late. Time is money!

On delivery day, the driver or van operator will contact you by phone to let you know that he or she is in the neighborhood and that you should be ready for acceptance. You will probably know approximately when you'll be receiving the call because you'll have agreed to a window of acceptance at your initial meeting.

It is important and also expected by the movers that you will take the time to show them around your home and flag special requests. You hired movers for their brawn, not their clairvoyant capabilities. Remember that the move will only be as smooth as your ability to communicate your wants and needs.

In other words, special instructions about placing the grand piano in the first floor foyer should be mentioned to the movers long before they're maneuvering it up your spiral staircase!

 ## Make a Date

Window of Delivery:

_____

_____

Once the movers arrive, expect to break out the big bills before your items are unloaded. If you've made special arrangements for a credit card payment, you will be expected to pay according to the terms established when you initially met with the moving agent.

Vital Statistics

Just like you were expected to produce cash upon arrival, it's typically the driver's job to give you the inventories that were prepared at your old home before the first box is budged.

Do not let the crew start unloading until you have these important documents in your hands!

Where Do You Want It Lady?

Even though you clearly marked all of your boxes with their room destinations, it's a good idea to map out the dimensions of each room before the movers arrive and make a log of where you want unmarked items, like beds, bicycles and boats.

Don't forget to decide ahead of time where table saws, Christmas trees and appliances will be placed. And don't make the mistake of avoiding this step and just having everything placed in the center of the living room, assuming that you'll take care of it later. Why break your back tomorrow when you've got muscles at your disposal today?

Candy…Cigars…Cigarettes

While we're not suggesting that you strap on a bustier and transform yourself into a cocktail waitress on moving day, at the very least have ice cold water and cups available for the movers.

Most companies have policies of non-acceptance of gratuities, including meals. However, it's best to ask your sales agent what is permissible and expected by the movers. In addition to cold drinks, show them where the bathrooms are located and have soap and towels on hand for cleanup.

They will expect to help themselves to these must-haves, so point out designated refresh stations ahead of time to keep the pace moving.

Where's My Washing Machine?

You could hold a swing dance in the back of the moving van—clearly your washing machine isn't hiding in a dark corner. Now what do you do?

Here's why that inventory sheet is so important! If any boxes, pieces of furniture or appliances are missing in action or were wounded in transit, make a note in the "exception column" on the inventory sheet.

This is your only protection. If you mark items as "received" and they're really "not received," Judge Judy will laugh you out of the courtroom when you attempt to recover expenses for your lost items.

Don't ditch your damaged boxes either. Remember, the moving company has the right to inspect damaged items and make their own notes and assessments. You may be forfeiting coverage if you toss the smoking gun in your complex's dumpster.

Check with your mover on claims procedures. Your course of action will be based upon the insurance plan you selected and paid for "back home."

Step Back

Sure, you're excited that you've made it to your new city and you'll be even giddier when you see that your pots and pans have too!

While you may be tempted to get your hands dirty and take on the role of moving apprentice, it's best to let the movers get their job done and for you to remain calm. Of course you should oversee the process and inform the movers of special requests, but stay out of their hair (and off the stairs) unless disaster is about to strike.

Movers are accustomed to anxious clients and will reassure you that things are under control. But remember, they will not have the same emotional connection that you have to your saltshaker collection. Don't be offended if they are uninterested in the life-size oil painting of your toddler posing with Mickey Mouse. They are there to get a job done—so let them do it!

If You're Doing It On Your Own...

Arrival At Your New Home

Before you break into the belly of the rental truck and organize the kids into an assembly line, take care of these priorities.

- ✓ Meet your real estate agent or stop by the leasing office at your new apartment to gather keys and sign leases and other important documents.
- ✓ Conduct a walk through of your new home or apartment. Whether you're renting property or will be making mortgage payments, make notes of items that are broken, missing or damaged.
- ✓ Contact utility companies to activate accounts.
- ✓ Ensure that utilities and appliances are in working order. Check the furnace, air conditioner, hot water heater and garbage disposal so you can call the Maytag Man if mayhem strikes.
- ✓ Determine if there are any priority cleaning, repairing or decorating tasks that should be done before furniture or boxes are in the way.

Call In the Troops

While you may feel like you need the help of the National Guard to get everything from the van actually into your home, you can accomplish great results with a little pre-planning.

Unless your dozen closest friends are moving along with you and your family, you'll need to get creative in soliciting helpers for moving day. Since you're moving to a brand new community, chances are good that you won't know the Bunkers across the street well enough to enlist their services. Consider these options instead for arranging an instant assembly line:

✓ Call your local United Way. With 1400 across the country, you'll likely find one in your new community. They'll be a great first start for providing a referral to a volunteer center, youth organization looking to accumulate service hours or agency sponsoring a work program. Locate your local United Way online at unitedway.org.

✓ Make a plea to your parish. Thinking about joining a church in your new community? What better way to learn more about your new home than to spend a day with a handful of church members. Contact the church office about a week prior to your arrival, explain your situation and you may just be surprised at the number of followers who respond to the "calling."

✓ Tap into temps. You know their names…why not get some man power from Manpower? Check your local yellow pages under "temporary agencies" and you're sure to find dozens in your new area.

✓ Hire high-schoolers. Contact a nearby high school and ask to talk to someone in the career services or student council office. You just might get in touch with some cheap labor!

Don't Lose Control

Moving day is not the time to get in touch with your shy side.

Your family and hired help will expect someone to be calling the shots, and that someone is you. Devise a plan so each person has a specific duty. Before your boxes see the light of day, huddle your helpers in one central location and go over the game plan.

Ideally, here's how it should work:

✓ Two adults should be assigned to in-truck duty. It's their job to get boxes and furniture safely out of the stacked pyramids and into the open arms of the ground crew.

✓ Hopefully your boxes are all marked with their room destinations in full view. This will make the job of the ground crew much easier. The last thing you want is the guy from the temp agency splitting open your box of toiletries just so he can decide where that box should go.

✓ If you'd rather be in the thick of things, assign a trusted teenager or senior as a helper at the front entrance. Let them know that they have the most important job of ticking off items on your inventory as each box and piece of furniture crosses the starting line into your new home.

You are the cruise director. That's right—you have the most important role of keeping everyone smiling (or at least not ripping each other's hair out), directing traffic, answering questions and facilitating the entire process.

 Make a Moving Memo

Furniture and where each piece will reside:

Item   Room

_____

_____

_____

_____

_____

_____

_____

_____

A Place to Keep My Notes and Reminders…

SECTION FIVE

Save Your Sanity

This section of *29 Days to a Smooth Move* looks at the emotion commotion that accompanies moving. Move your pets and kids without tearing your hair out. Stop and say goodbye to all you've known. Finally, dream a little dream about what good things are bound to happen next!

Chapter 17:
An Ocean Of Emotion
Your mind may be keeping busy with all you have to do before the move, but how's your heart coping? If you're anything like most of us, it's doing its share of flip-flops at the thought of moving.

It's important not to pack your feelings right along with the fine china. Instead, reflect on what you're going through and your reactions to it. And, just like packing, this process is not going to take care of itself overnight. In the meantime, get started with some of our thought-provoking ideas of what you might be feeling—and how you're going to handle it.

Chapter 18:
Saying Goodbye: It's a Family Affair
Bidding adieu to those you love can be one of the most trying parts of moving. Those farewells usually come at about the same time as some of the more stressful moments—like right after you packed up a 25-foot semi tractor trailer with nearly every possession you own!

There are ways to get through it—and even grow in the process. This chapter will explain the spiritual value of formally saying goodbye to the family, friends and even places you've grown to love.

Chapter 19:
Take This Job…
You may have been dreaming of this moment for years—strutting into your boss's office and saying, somewhat louder than necessary, "I quit!"

Well, it's probably better to keep that particular scenario in your dreams. Even if you're moving to take the best job ever created, it's a good idea to use some tact when you're parting ways with your soon-to-be former company. Here's everything you need to know to do just that!

Chapter 20:
Don't Have a Cow, Dude! Children and Teens on the Move

No doubt about it—kids take moving hard.

We're sure you can remember the great traumas of child- and teenhood: Doing homework, making friends and finding zits. It's no fun leaving the known behind and becoming "the new kid" in one fell swoop.

This chapter helps you help your children from the announcement to the transition—especially when trying to communicate to your teen, even in those times you may not recognize him or her!

Chapter 21:
Moving the Whole "Kitten" Caboodle (And Poochie Patoodle!)

In the best of times, pets help you remain calm, cool and collected. In moving times, you may enter another emotional dimension altogether.

In fact, this could get kinda hairy.

Don't despair, after reading this chapter, you'll be ready to move a zoo if you have to!

Chapter 22:
Every Exit Is an Entrance Someplace Else

Praise be, you're done! Or are you just beginning? Welcome to your fresh start. Knees knocking a little? Don't worry, it happens to the best of us. Discover how moving can truly fuel your dreams. Your new life is waiting—act now!

Chapter 17

An Ocean of Emotion

There's no doubt about it—moving brings on an onslaught of emotions. You might be feeling...

- ✓ Excited about your new beginning
- ✓ Guilty about leaving friends and family behind
- ✓ Apprehensive about the unknowns of a new community
- ✓ Overwhelmed with questions about where your life is going
- ✓ Sad about separating yourself from all you know

It's perfectly normal to be feeling these emotions and others. There's more than the physical aspect to moving—your mind is turned upside down, too!

Along those same lines, you and your family aren't the only ones experiencing upheaval. Friends and family staying behind are going through their share of thoughts and emotions. If you put yourself in their shoes, you'd realize they might be feeling...

- ✓ Worried about your adventure
- ✓ Anxious about life without you
- ✓ Sad you're leaving
- ✓ Overly thrilled for you (raise an eyebrow at this one!)
- ✓ Even jealous because you're moving on

With some thought and preparation, you can work through the emotions surrounding your move a little easier.

We're the first to say it, we're not therapists! But we know a little bit of thought and journaling can go a long way to helping you feel better about the changes going on around you.

First, spend some time thinking about your own feelings. Even if you're excited about your move, it will be tempered by stages of sadness and anxiety. Allow yourself to feel these emotions. It doesn't mean you're not happy about your new beginning. It means you're human.

 ## Make a Moving Memo

Identify the feelings you have about your move:

I feel…

_____

_____

_____

_____

_____

_____

_____

Things can be even tougher if you're not happy about your move, say if it's forced due to a spouse changing jobs or other reasons. Again, perfectly natural. Allow yourself to feel angry and grieve over your loss, but still work to stabilize your emotions and thoughts and move towards acceptance.

For instance, if you're heartbroken about leaving friends and family behind, map out how you will stay in touch by visiting in three months or with frequent e-mails and calls.

Identify the positives and negatives about your move:

Make a Moving Memo

I'm happy about moving because:

_____

_____

_____

_____

_____

_____

_____

_____

"I'm not so thrilled" and "am feeling blue" about moving because:

_____

_____

_____

_____

_____

_____

_____

_____

Bringing forward awareness is the first step. Besides writing the feelings down in your moving manual, you can also talk to a friend or family member about your fears. Perhaps seek counseling from a member of the clergy. The important thing is to admit first to yourself, and then to others, your fears. Then those fears become much easier to deal with.

Make a Moving Memo

My moving hang-ups and ideas about how to solve them:

_____

_____

_____

_____

_____

_____

_____

_____

Houston, We Have a Problem

In the movie *Apollo 13*, the engineers and scientists at Houston's Mission Control were letting "stinkin' thinkin'" get the best of them when three astronauts became stranded in space. Mission Control leader Gene Krantz, portrayed by Ed Harris, would have none of it. "Work the problem, people!" he said.

Sometimes we're facing problems and situations that are out of our control. But what's important people is how we "work the problem." (Incidentally, if you haven't seen the movie, it's very inspiring. We suggest you watch it while you pack.)

The above suggestions can also be modified and used when talking to your children and teens about their fears with moving.

If you look hard enough, you can find a silver lining to the sad cloud and make peace with your decision to move. But, if it's just not working for you, do seek professional help.

A Place To Keep My Notes and Reminders…

Chapter 18

Saying Goodbye—It's a Family Affair

Hear Ye! Hear Ye!

If you're moving out of the area, telling friends and family about your plans may be one of the hardest parts of your move. It takes some time and adjustment on both sides—yours and theirs. But, like the rest of your move, some planning and organization will get you through it.

Establish a Script

Think about how you will tell them and when. There are many ways to do it. Individually or a family meeting. On the phone, in person or by e-mail.

- ✓ Whatever you do, don't tell everyone by yelling out the window of the moving van on your way out of town. Letting friends and family know in advance will give them the time they need to process their own feelings and say goodbye.

- ✓ Some friends and family will want to hear all the details. For those who want to know what's going on, keep them in the loop. Moving doesn't only involve you, it involves them as well.

- ✓ Other friends and family members may become withdrawn and quiet. Be patient and let them know you're there if and when they want to talk about your pending departure.

Tara's Tale—

Digging Our Grave on Memorial Day

It was a dark and stormy day, the afternoon of Memorial Day 2001 to be exact. We were invited to my aunt's house and the tension mounted as Ron and I nudged each other under the makeshift indoor picnic table.

Once the hotdogs were gone, we nervously made our moving announcement. My cousin cried, my aunt was speechless and my Grandma declared, "Now I only have six grandchildren!" (My sister quickly reminded her that I wasn't dead yet!)

 Make a Moving Memo

How I will announce my move:

_____

_____

_____

_____

_____

_____

_____

C'mon—Say It!

Okay, you've told everybody. Unfortunately, it's not the end of the emotional trauma. For your mental health and well being, we highly suggest that, unless you're running from the law, don't sneak out of town without saying goodbye.

Unless you've been a real hermit, you have to bid farewell to:

✓ Family
✓ Friends
✓ Co-workers
✓ Neighbors
✓ Your vital service providers, such as the person who cuts your hair just the right way…(That can be a mighty tearful farewell!)

With some of them, your moving announcement can be followed by a simple "goodbye" and that's the end of it. Oh, if it only were so easy with everybody else!

Tara's Tale—

A Surprise Visitor

Ron and I got the surprise of our life on Moving Day Eve when my brother-in-law Ray of Boston magically appeared for an in-person goodbye. If we didn't hug him with our own arms, we wouldn't have believed it! It was one of the most meaningful things anyone has ever done for us. Lesson learned: For those unexpected emotional surprises in the days leading up to departure, have plenty of Kleenex available!

Saying Goodbye To Friends and Family

Goodbye parties take the cake when it comes to saying farewell. You can gather everyone together for an exciting afternoon or evening of moving anticipation, excitement and fond farewells.

Here are some ideas for your shindig:

✓ Have stacks of cards with your new address and phone number placed where people congregate.
✓ Ask guests to "sign in" by filling in contact information in your address book.

✓ Place several disposable cameras around to snap some happy memories of your party.

✓ Keep the menu simple so you have time to mingle.

Donna's Ditty—

It's My Party...

Sixty people crowded into my two-bedroom apartment in Erie to bid me a fond farewell before my move to sunny San Diego. I made two huge crock-pots of soup and offered bread and cake. That, plus a refrigerator well-stocked with beer, wine and champagne, had everybody feeling happy for me one way or another!

With friends and family still talking about it years later, my "Goodbye Party" put a happy ending to all my years in the Erie area—I highly recommend throwing yourself a similar celebration event.

Tara's Tale—

So Long, Farewell, Auf Weidersehen, Goodnight!

To overcome our anxieties about saying goodbye, Ron and I celebrated ourselves and let others do the same. Instead of resisting farewell parties, we basked in the friendships we had made over the years.

We let our parents treat us to "going away" dinners at overpriced restaurants and agreed to the silly stunts and charades that our co-workers insisted upon as they sent us on our way. We realized that the festivities were as important for us as they were for our hosts.

Don't leave your kids out of this important process, either. Make cupcakes for the class and let them have a chance to say goodbye to their buds with a special going away celebration.

Goodbye Porch, Goodbye Kitchen, Goodbye Bathroom

Just as it's important to bid farewell to friends and family, it's also important to say goodbye to your house and neighborhood.

- ✓ Take a break from packing and take a leisurely tour of your home to remember the good times.
- ✓ Snap some photos of your favorite spots. Get them developed before you leave and tuck them in this manual.
- ✓ Say a prayer of thanksgiving for your shelter followed by a prayer of peace to those who will reside there next.

Tara's Tale—

Goodbye, Sweet Closet

While I knew moving day would bring a bundle of emotions, I never thought I'd be sharing my soft side with a 3'x 7' closet.

But, there I was standing in the middle of our unique bedroom closet—the one with the little window in it. Just months before I had emptied every last shoe out to paint the space a warm shade of buttercup with purple and green trim to match the bedroom. I even made a valance for the little window.

This was no closet—it was my creation! Between swallowed tears, I managed to smile for a Kodak moment and with one click, my mini moving day breakdown in the closet earned its place into the history book of our life.

 **Make a Moving Memo**

For my goodbye ceremonies, I will:

_____

_____

_____

_____

_____

_____

_____

Donna's Ditty—

Good to the Last Drop

It may seem uncomfortable, but a goodbye ceremony really helps soothe the soul. For about 15 minutes the day before I moved, I drank a large mug of coffee while meditating on the snow falling on State Street in Erie. I tuned into what was inside and listened to what it had to say in appreciation for my apartment and the good times I had there. It was a simple ceremony, yet effective.

Tara's Tale—

A Final Salute

It rivaled the stomach-in-the-throat pomp and circumstance of the Changing of the Guard at the Tomb of the Unknown Soldier. It was Moving Day. 5:45 a.m. With tear-filled eyes and wet cheeks we locked the back door of our little brick home in Erie for the last time.

In cadence, we marched to the 18-foot flag pole in our front yard. Slowly, ceremoniously, Ron unhoisted the Stars and Stripes that had been given to us a wedding gift. Bawling, we gave it a good old-fashioned Boy Scout fold, tucked it behind the driver's seat and pulled out of Post Avenue for the last time ever.

Your departure may not be quite as formal, but do remember to turn around and say goodbye to your abode—it served you well!

There's Still Work to Do

Unfortunately, these ceremonies won't totally banish the homesickness you're bound to feel in the days, weeks and even months following your move.

Both of us went through this.

They say it takes about a year, but it actually took Donna two before she could really call San Diego home. Despite all that California has to offer, there were moments where she missed Pennsylvania—with its green summer days and crisp winter evenings—terribly.

But as she grew to "know" her new community, those feelings dissipated until eventually "home" meant San Diego, not Erie. She really started coming into her own when she joined a new church where she attended classes and made friends left and right. It offered her a safe community where she blossomed and discovered how much more she had to offer herself and others.

After a few months in Vegas, Tara told herself she was perfectly well-adjusted—until she unexpectedly spent one evening crying uncontrollably into her pillow because she missed her parents so much after their Thanksgiving visit. It's true what they say about a good cry—you feel so much better afterwards! It's also true that time helps heal all wounds, and it wasn't long before Tara and Ron were loving life in Las Vegas.

We're not going to kid you, moving takes its toll on your emotions. But don't be frightened of them. Embrace your emotions as a learning and growing process—no matter what your age!

A Place To Keep My Notes and Reminders…

Chapter 19

Take This Job...

Even if you're moving a million miles away, take Donna's grandfather's advice and "stay on everybody's good side."

In today's world of telecommuting, you never know when you'll have opportunity to work for the company via phone and computer!

Donna's Ditty—

Live, From San Diego

For a time, I was busier after I left work than before!

During the day I was looking for a place to live in San Diego and at night I was completing annual report work for the company I left behind. I appreciated the freelance work—it gave me some income while I changed my life around. It also paved the way for more freelance work for my former company, which eventually led me to the decision to become a full-time freelance writer.

How To Leave Your Job

Determine when your last day will be and do your best to give ample notice to your boss. Although it's not the law, it's common practice to give at least two weeks' notice, which most people consider the minimum. If you can't give at least two weeks' notice, explain why (briefly) in your resignation letter and tell your boss in person.

Make a Date

Give notice: _____

Exit interview: _____

Last day on the job: _____

Parting Is Such Sweet Sorrow...

Your letter of resignation should be short and simple. Here's a sample:

"I am resigning my position as marketing manager at Mom's Moonpies effective July 1 of this year."

Easy, right?

If you like, you can add a little something pleasant about your time with Mom's Moonpies: "I appreciate the time and opportunities presented to me here and consider it 'one small step for me, one big step for my career.'"

(But remember, like Mom always said, if you can't say something nice...)

Sign it and you're done.

Telling the Boss

Letter in hand, it's time to let your boss in on your plans. Hopefully this will be a pleasant and positive experience for you. Again, keep it simple and civil. Tell your supervisor when, where and why you're leaving. Your parting words should be positive, not bitter.

If you *have* to speak your mind about problems with the company, its management or your job, request a more formal exit interview on your last day of work to air your grievances and give your former company some valuable information.

Last but not least, follow up with the human resources department to make sure you get all that is coming to you in unused vacation pay, and retirement or pension money. Also, return whatever belongs to the company, such as its car and laptop, in good working order.

 ## Make a Moving Memo

Things to return to my soon-to-be former workplace:

_____

_____

_____

_____

_____

_____

_____

Things of mine to retrieve from my workplace:

_____

_____

_____

_____

_____

_____

_____

And remember to say goodbye to your coworkers and workplace as well—they've no doubt been a bit part of you life!

Tara's Tale—

Up, Up and Away!

On our last day of work, Ron and I celebrated the next chapter of our lives with a balloon launch from the top of the tower on the docks of Lake Erie. Armed with cherry red helium balloons three times the size of our heads, we each made a wish and...poof...they were gone. (Although it would have been more picture perfect if Mother Nature blew our balloons in the direction of Las Vegas instead of Buffalo!)

Want Practical Advice on Finding a Job?

Like our style and want our insights into finding a new job? Then read our book *Get A Job: Put Your Degree To Work*. We've included a sample chapter in the back of this book, and you can find out more at getajobbook.com.

A Place to Keep My Notes and Reminders...

Chapter 20

Don't Have a Cow, Dude!
Children and Teens on the Move

Let's face it—moving isn't just about you. If you share the house with a spouse or some offspring, it's about them too.

Moving upsets routines and balances. It causes a slew of emotions to emerge. From tykes to teens, kids feel the stress of a move just as much, if not more, than adults. They frequently feel their world is being spun out of control.

Some typical reactions:

- ✓ "I finally got the lead in the school play—and you're saying we're moving?"
- ✓ "I finally made the cheerleading squad—and you're making me move?"
- ✓ "I finally got a girlfriend—and we're moving?"

But, there's no question about it, you're moving. Even though you're making the final decision, don't run roughshod over your children's feelings.

Breaking the News

First, break the news to family members gently. Tell them what they need to know and what will help them understand the reason for the move.

They may not like it, but your reasoning will help them understand the purpose behind the turmoil. You know your kids and probably have a good idea how they'll react. Rehearse how you'll break the news, what you'll tell them and what you can do to make the situation easier for them. If possible, include them in the decision making process up front—even if their vote won't really count!

Easy With the Young Kiddies

If you have very young children, you've been given a nice break and little less trauma to deal with. The youngest children only need to know that Mommy and Daddy have to move to a new workplace or a new town, or to be closer to an older relative. Home is everything to very young children. To lessen their anxiety, you may want to put off telling them until you have to begin packing.

For elementary school children, alert the teacher of your upcoming move in case your kid's friends and class would like to say a formal goodbye to their mate.

Also, reassure your kids with the fact that they will be able to keep in touch with their buddies through e-mail, letters and the phone. If your move doesn't take you too far away, establish a "visit weekend" and invite your child's friends to visit the new locale.

And lend a helping hand to establish new relationships for your child. Contact your new community's school principal to see if there are any children your kid's age who would e-mail your youngin' and maybe show him or her the ropes on the first couple days of class.

Brace Yourself For The Teens

Older children and young teens need—and deserve—to know more. Although they may not like it, eventually they can understand the reasons for the move.

For older children, here's one way to handle the news in the least spastic way possible:

- ✓ After uttering the words "We're moving," be prepared to back up your announcement with a list of advantages to the new location, such as a better school, new sports or a huge mall. (But don't go overboard. Is the phrase "Gag me with a spoon, Mom!" still around?)

- ✓ Be ready for some shrill screaming, sullen silences and stomping scenarios—kids don't take change lightly.

- ✓ To pleas of "Why, why, why?" answer these and other questions as fully as you can and with patience and understanding.

✓ Keep your chin—and spirits—up. Hopefully your attitude will be catching.

✓ Reassure your child that you will do what you can to help them with the transition.

✓ Make it a family effort and involve them in the packing process, house selection and learning about your new community.

✓ Arrange a tour or at least a drive-by of their new school and other areas where they may be hanging out, like the YMCA and baseball fields.

✓ Keep your kids up to date on plans and tasks, and, to the greatest extent possible, involved. Let them help make some of the decisions and even take them house hunting with you, if you can.

✓ Show children your new home in advance of the move or at least as soon as you arrive. Help them pick out their rooms so they can begin establishing their own space.

More Tips for Teens

Teens, especially, finding moving difficult because their young lives revolve around friends, places and activities outside your home. Picking them up and plopping them in a new location takes some finesse.

✓ Make time for your teen. Moving is stressful and time consuming, but take time to talk to your teen and empathize with his or her concerns.

✓ Go out of your way to try to help with the transition. If you have a choice, move during the summer so your teen begins the school year fresh and, if you're lucky, with some other "newbies."

✓ Sometimes the best way to get involved is to jump right in, feet first! Encourage your children to seek out activities and interest in the new location, be it the stamp club or rugby team. Hopefully it won't take too long 'til they're "one of the crowd." (Remember this advice for yourself, too!)

✓ Don't recognize your teen because of the neon pink hair and plethora of studs? Sometimes teens lash out against authority by doing something special just to push your buttons. Patience, people, patience! It's difficult, but the best thing to do is close your eyes to the new tattoo and instead, concentrate on talking and listening to your teen to determine what's *really* trying to be said.

✓ By the same token, your teens may be trying to push you to see how much you'll give. They may actually want you to assert some discipline and play your parental role by laying down some ground rules and not giving in to their every desire. How do you do that? Sorry—that's another book in itself!

It's Not Working

The transition doesn't end when the boxes are unpacked (or still full up in the attic). It takes some time (sometimes a year or two) for you and your kids to become adjusted to new surroundings.

If that time goes by and you or your children are still feeling unsettled, seek professional help to address any problems brought on by the move or its effects. And, if you're moving the family because of a divorce or death, your children could benefit from counseling even more.

A Place to Keep My Notes and Reminders…

Chapter 21

Moving the Whole "Kitten" Caboodle (And Poochie Patoodle!)

Should you even take the dog and cat?

"Not take the cat and dog? Are you crazy?!"

That's what we thought you'd say. So here's a whole section on moving your pets to a new location.

Before the Move, Watch For Signs of Apprehension

Furry family members might be going through their own moving anxiety. Pay attention to changes in their eating and sleeping habits. Yes, there are a million things to do, but try to take some time out to play with Rover and reassure him that even though everything is going topsy-turvy around him, he still has your love.

Donna's Ditty—

My Cat Needs Rogaine

Be alert to changes in behavior. When I moved from my farmhouse to an apartment in Erie, my cat Baby took a long look at all the new boxes and then started losing (and, unfortunately, eating) her hair.

After diagnosing an intestinal blockage that was easily fixed with a shot and some pills, the vet asked if there were some changes going on in the household that would cause my cat to freak out. Seems that a zillion empty boxes plus a distracted and slightly frantic owner were enough to alert my little cat that big changes were in the works.

Keep tabs on your tabby so the same doesn't happen to you!

Spend a little extra time cuddling the kitty or doggy to reassure them that life is going to be okay.

Away On Moving Day

On moving day, it's best to keep pets out of the way. See if they can stay at a friend's house or board them.

Another option is to keep dogs crated (if they are used to it—not a good idea if they aren't) and cats shut up in one room. Better a day of stress for the domesticated beasties instead of days, weeks or months of heartache if the pet gets out and runs away.

 Make a Moving Memo

Vet Checklist:

- ☐ Records
- ☐ Vaccinations
- ☐ Treatments
- ☐ Tranquilizers

Do Professional Movers Take Pets?

You wish! No, federal regulations prohibit moving companies from shipping animals in moving vans. Besides, pets—like plants—travel best under your own care.

Pet Travel Prep

✓ Carry health and rabies certificates with you. Airlines and state health officials generally require health certificates for all animals transported by air. In most cases, health certificates must be issued by a licensed veterinarian examining the animal within 10 days of transport.

✓ Ask your veterinarian to provide any required vaccinations and treatments. Does your pet have appropriate heartworm protection if the mosquito season begins earlier or ends later in the area you will be moving to?

Administer tranquilizers with the prescribed dosage only if specifically prescribed by your veterinarian.

✓ Pack your pets' water and food bowls, grooming equipment and any medication they may require. To avoid digestive upsets, take a supply of their favorite dry food with you.

Turn Your Head and Cough

Interstate health certificates must be obtained for dogs and horses prior to entering most states. Nearly all states require a rabies vaccine for dogs, and many require them for cats. If you're lucky enough to be moving to Hawaii, keep in mind that the state requires that cats and dogs be quarantined for 120 days.

If your move is across state lines, call or write to the state veterinarian, state department of animal husbandry or other authority for more information.

Fido, the Backseat Driver

Thinking about taking your pet in the car? First, make sure he's healthy and, second, make sure he will be a good traveler.

If you haven't already, accustom your pet to riding in your car. Begin with short rides each day and gradually increase the length of each ride. If your pet is unable to adjust to short rides, consider plane travel.

Here's how you can keep your pet comfortable and safe on the road.

✓ Do not feed your pet for at least three hours before leaving on a trip. Take your dog for a walk just before your start the drive. You will still have to stop along the way, but your dog will be more comfortable as the trip gets underway.

✓ During stops, provide fresh drinking water for your dog. You may also reward it with a dog snack for being a good traveler.

✓ If the drive is eight hours or longer, give your cat the opportunity to use a litter pan and offer it fresh drinking water.

✓ Feed your pet shortly after you arrive at your destination or when you have stopped for the day.

Here's what to put in your pet travel kit: food, water, dishes, can opener (if needed), leash, a few treats, favorite toy and some type of bedding. Don't forget a scooper and plastic bags for cleanup!

One King or Two Queens?

There are a growing number of pet-friendly hotels on the road. You'll find a very handy resource in petswelcome.com, where you can search by city for hotels, B&B's—even amusement parks—that are pet friendly. Visit the site and plan your route so that reservations are made in advance for you—and your pet! Just click on their "listings" section to start your search.

Fluffy, the Co-Pilot

What are restrictions on air travel with dogs and cats?

No airline will guarantee acceptance of an animal it has not seen. Important considerations for acceptance of animals include the health and disposition of the animal, proper health certificates and kennel markings and sizing.

Airlines also require that wheels installed as part of a kennel be removed or rendered inoperable prior to transport. This action prevents kennels from turning the plane's cargo area into a roller rink. USDA assigns airlines the final responsibility for determining the safety and compliance of the kennels they accept.

Airlines generally transport animals in the cargo compartment of a plane. In doing so, the airlines advise the flight crew that animals are onboard the aircraft. Some airlines allow passengers to carry their pets in the cabin of a plane if the animals are capable of fitting under the passenger's seat. (Carry-on pets are not protected under the Animal Welfare Act.)

Certain animals are accepted as baggage at passenger check-in locations, and others are accepted as cargo at the airline cargo facilities. For the specific requirements pertaining to your animal, make advance arrangements with the airline you are using.

Airlines must ensure that they have facilities to handle animals at the airports of transfer and final destination. Airlines must comply with USDA-APHIS guidelines on allowable temperature limits for animal-holding areas.

Finally, airlines are not required to carry live animals, and they reserve the right to refuse to carry an animal for any reason.

 Make a Moving Memo

The airlines I'm considering and their pet rules:

_____

_____

_____

_____

_____

_____

_____

_____

For a Smooth Flight

- ✓ Try to avoid peak travel periods when delays and stopovers are longer. Plan a trip with as few stops and transfers as possible. Avoid traveling in extremely hot or cold weather to avoid dangerous loading and unloading periods for your pet.

- ✓ When you make your reservation, tell the airline directly that you will have an animal with you. Be sure to reconfirm with the airline 24 to 48 hours before departure that you will bring your pet. Advance arrangements are not a guarantee that your animal will travel on a specific flight.

✓ Arrive at the airport with plenty of time to spare. If your animal is traveling as a carry-on pet or by the special expedited delivery service, check-in will typically be at the passenger terminal.

✓ If you are sending your pet through the cargo system, you'll need to go to the cargo terminal, usually located in a separate part of the airport. Note that by regulation an animal may be presented for transport no more than four hours before flight time.

✓ Some airlines allow cats and small dogs to travel (generally for an additional charge) with their owner if the carrier fits under the passenger seat. Otherwise, rent or purchase a carrier or crate that meets airline regulations and affix a LIVE ANIMAL sticker. Mark it with your name and address and the name of a person who can be contacted about your pet at your destination, if necessary.

✓ Put a cushion or blanket on the crate floor. Attach a water cup to the crate door. The cup should be deep, but not too full of water to avoid spilling.

✓ On the day of the flight, take your dog for a long walk before leaving for the airport.

✓ At the end of your trip, pick up your pet promptly.

Kennel Constraints

Dogs and cats must be at least eight weeks old and must have been weaned before traveling by air. Kennels must meet minimum standards for size, strength, sanitation and ventilation.

Size and Strength

Kennels must be enclosed and allow room for the animal to stand, sit and lie in a natural position. They must be easy to open, strong enough to withstand the normal rigors of transportation and free of objects that could injure the animal.

Sanitation

Kennels must have a solid, leak proof floor that is covered with litter or absorbent lining. Wire or other ventilated sub-floors are generally allowed; pegboard flooring is prohibited.

Ventilation

Kennels must be well ventilated with openings that make up at least 14 percent of the total wall space. At least one third of the openings must be located in the top half of the kennel. Kennels also must have rims to prevent ventilation openings from being blocked by other cargo. These rims—usually placed on the sides of the kennel—must provide at least three quarters of an inch clearance.

Grips and Markings

Kennels must have grips or handles for lifting to prevent cargo personnel from having to place their fingers inside the kennel and risk being bitten. Kennels also must be marked "live animals" or "wild animals" on the top and one side with directional arrows indicating proper position of the kennel. Lettering must be at least 1 inch high.

Animals Per Kennel

Each species must have its own kennel, with the exception of compatible cats and dogs of similar size. Maximum numbers include two puppies or kittens under six months old—20 pounds each and of similar size, 15 guinea pigs or rabbits and 50 hamsters.

Donna's Ditty—

Tickets for Two, Please

Some airlines may have more restrictive requirements, such as allowing only one adult animal per kennel or, as I found out, "two cats per plane" when they are flying in the cabin. Be sure to check with the airline you're using before trying to move your menagerie in one trip.

Peanuts? Pretzels?

Instructions for feeding and watering your pet over a 24-hour period must be attached to the kennel. This 24-hour schedule will assist the airline in providing care for your animal in case it is diverted from its original destination.

Food and water dishes must be securely attached and accessible to caretakers without opening the kennel. Food and water must be provided to puppies and kittens every 12 hours until they are 16 weeks old. Mature animals must be fed every 24 hours and given water every 12 hours.

If Your Pet Turns Up Missing

If your pet should turn up missing during transport, immediately speak to airline personnel. Many airlines have computer tracking systems that can trace a pet transferred to an incorrect flight. If there is no report of your animal, proceed with these steps:

✓ Contact animal control agencies and humane societies in the local and surrounding areas. Check with them daily.

✓ Contact the APHIS-Animal Care regional office closest to where your pet was lost. Eastern Region: (301) 734-4981, Central Region: (817) 885-6910, Western Region: (916) 857-6205. For further information, call 1-800-545-USDA.

✓ Provide descriptions and photographs to the airline, local animal control agencies and humane societies. Help can also be sought from radio stations. Leave telephone numbers and addresses with all these locations should you have to return home.

✓ You can also contact the Missing Pet Network (missingpet.net). Follow the advice on "How to post a listing." The MPN is a group of volunteers sponsored by the USDA Animal Care Office.

ID Your Pet

Securing identification is one of the most important preparations you can make.

Be sure your pet's identification tags are securely attached. Attach tags to your pet's collar or leg band (for birds). ID tags should include your pet's name, your name, address and phone number, destination address and phone number. Most states also require dogs and cats to have a rabies tag on their collars.

Take color pictures of your pet and make a written description of its colorings and distinguishing marks. Record your pet's body size and weight. If your pet is lost, these identification aids could make the difference in locating it.

Your Feathered Friends

Birds and small pets, such as gerbils and hamsters, can generally travel in their cages in the car. Birds are very susceptible to drafts and sudden changes in temperature, as well as being easily frightened. To keep your bird calm, its cage should be covered while on the road.

Remove the water container from the cage to avoid spills. Place the cage in the car out of drafts but with plenty of ventilation, and be sure it will not tip over. Give the pet fresh water at every stop as small pets become dehydrated very quickly, particularly during hot weather. Feed at normal intervals.

There you have it—how to move your pet in, oh, a hundred easy steps! Again, remember that preparation and organization is key. Do your homework and things go a lot smoother!

A Place to Keep My Notes and Reminders…

Chapter 22

Every Exit Is an Entrance Somewhere Else

Finished!

Bet you never want to go through that again!

Odds are, however, you just might! Statistics say the average American moves nearly every five years—and that number does indeed take into consideration all those people who are happy living in the same place their entire lives. Amazing!

Before you begin planning your next moving venture, you might as well see what this place has to offer, right?

Donna's Ditty—

Is This It?

I remember my first days in San Diego. There was a part of my mind that simply remained in moving mode. It worked on where to get boxes, what to look for in a new place and what I would do when I got there. It wasn't that I wasn't happy with my move, I just missed the excitement of working out the logistics.

When I realized what was happening, I gave that part of me something new to work on—including finding work!

There's a certain adrenalin rush that comes with moving—you can't expect that rush to leave just because everything is done. Instead, use those well-developed skills of organization to tackle the next project needed to make your new house (or apartment, or condo) a home.

A New Beginning

Changing location means changing your outlook—hopefully for the better! Besides cleaning out your closets, moving gives you an opportunity to empty your mind and body of bad habits—and build on some dreams.

And maybe, just maybe, go a little crazy by going by a new name or changing the color of your hair. Who's to know the difference?

Got some habits you'd love to leave behind? You don't have to take them with you. Your boxes are sealed anyway so toss them out with the rest of the trash!

 Make a Moving Memo

Habits, routines and other things I'd really rather leave behind:

_____

_____

_____

_____

_____

_____

Out with the old and in with the new—now's the time to add some more healthy routines to your lifestyle.

Aim high and kickoff your new life as a non-smoker who doesn't eat between meals, meditates every morning, flosses every night and exercises for 60 minutes every afternoon.

Make a Moving Memo

New routines I welcome into my life:

_____

_____

_____

_____

_____

_____

Have you ever mused over an idea and then dismissed it with the mantra "Someday. Someday." Well, someday has arrived, my friend! There's no time like the present to act on that dream!

C'mon—there must be something you always wanted to do! Now's your chance to:

- ✓ Pursue your latent passion for painting.
- ✓ Hi Ho, Silver! Hop on that horse and sample life as a cowgirl.
- ✓ Take up yoga and balance your life!

If you set your move in motion to get a new lease on life, make it so. Design a life more aligned to what you always hoped it would be. Take what you need and leave the rest.

Can you ever go back and visit the old 'hood? Of course! But don't be surprised if things there change, too. It's all part of transitions and the cycle of life. Wipe away those tears, because you'll always have your memories!

Tara's Tale—

Wall-to-Wall Distress

It was our first visit back to the old neighborhood. Slowly, cautiously I directed Ron around the bend of the corner lot where "our" snow-covered house sat smiling. "HIT THE BRAKES!" Do my eyes deceive me or are those antique white walls that I see through the parted curtains? After a near cardiac arrest, I gained composure, wiped away the tears that spontaneously flooded my face and made peace with the fact that the new owner had the right to redecorate, even if our sage walls DID look sharper…

At least the kitchen cupboards were still painted green.

As you close this moving manual and open up the next chapter of your life, remember one thing…

> **"It is good to have an end to journey towards;**
> **but it is the journey that matters, in the end."**
> —Ursula K. LeGuin

Okay, okay, we know it's corny, but we went 21 chapters strong without getting philosophical! The moral of this story is to have nothing but fun! We wish you wide smiles and smooth moves in the 29 days ahead.

Donna Kozik   Tara Maras

A Place To Keep My Notes and Reminders…

BONUS

29 Days to a Smooth Move Calendar and Checklist

As Soon as You Know You're Moving

☐ **Count and Toss**

Create an inventory of household goods and begin to declutter by beginning with the "non-living" areas, such as the basement, attic and garage.

☐ **Eat Up**

Use foods and cleaning supplies that can't be moved.

☐ **Put a Value On It**

For insurance reasons, have your home's antiques, pieces of art and other valuables appraised.

☐ **The Final Exam**

Arrange to transfer school records as needed.

☐ **Check Up**

Get dental cleanings, pay a visit to the doctor, take the pets to the vet, etc. Ask the professionals for referrals.

☐ **Me or Them?**

Look into reserving a rental truck or begin seeking estimates from professional movers.

☐ **File It!**

Create a place for all your moving paperwork, such as estimates, receipts, contracts, floor plans, etc.

☐ **Make It Official**

Drop by the local post office for a few sets of change-of-address cards and start notifying magazines, creditors and others of your move. (A lot of this can be done online—yay!)

The Next 28 Days (Give or Take) Before Moving Day

☐ **Pack the Halls**

Collect packing materials and box items you won't need until after you arrive at your new home.

☐ **Give Me Room**

Set up a packing area by emptying a room, the garage or a large space.

☐ **Power to the People**

Touch base with phone, power and other utilities services so they disconnect at your old home and connect your new one.

☐ **From Here to There**

Make the travel plans necessary to get you from one location to the next!

☐ **Getting Covered**

Call your insurance agent and verify that your possessions will be covered during transit.

☐ **Fido a Go-Go**

Set up transport of your pets and plants.

Three Weeks Before Moving Day

☐ **Let's Make a Deal**

Have your moving sale.

☐ **Give a Gift**

Contact area charities for pickup of unwanted items—don't forget to get a donation receipt for taxes.

☐ **Watch Over Them**

Make child care arrangements for moving day.

☐ **My Mantra: Get Rid of It**

Dispose of items that cannot be moved, such as flammable liquids.

Two Weeks Before Moving Day

☐ **What's Yours Is Yours…**
Return library books and other borrowed items.

☐ **What's Mine Is Mine**
Collect any loaned items.

☐ **Lube and Oil Change**
Service your car in preparation for the move.

☐ **Refill the Scripts**
Transfer prescriptions and medical records and make sure you have an adequate supply to see you through a week or two in your new location.

One Week Before Moving Day

☐ **Take the Key**
Close your safety deposit box.

☐ **Make the Switch**
Transfer your bank accounts.

☐ **Where's the Tape?**
If you're doing it yourself, finish up packing.

☐ **Here, Kitty, Kitty!**
Take animals to the vet for immunizations, if necessary.

☐ **Spring a Leak**
Drain lawn equipment of oil and gas and empty all water hoses.

☐ **Got the tickets?**
Confirm travel reservations.

☐ **Ice Breaker**
Defrost refrigerator and freezer.

☐ **Mickey Dis-mantle**
Disconnect and prepare major appliances for move.

☐ **Separate the Goods**
Put aside anything that will travel in your car or on the plane so that it will not be loaded on the truck.

☐ **Don't Forget the Coffee!**
Pack a box of necessary items that will be needed for the first day in the new place.

☐ **Got Cash?**
Get money or travelers' checks for the trip and to pay the movers.

☐ **When You Gonna Be There?**
Confirm the time the moving van will arrive.

☐ **Tear It Down**
If moving yourself, take apart beds and other large furniture.

Moving Out Day

☐ **Anybody Home?**
Make sure someone's around the house to answer the movers' questions.

☐ **Study the Small Print**
If using a mover, read your bill of lading and inventory carefully before signing. Keep the paperwork in a safe place.

☐ **Just in Case**
Jot down all utility meter readings.

Moving In Day

☐ **Pay Up**
Be prepared to pay your mover with cash, certified check or travelers' check unless other arrangements have been made in advance.

☐ **Give Them a Good Looksee**
Check your belongings carefully and note on the inventory of boxes if anything was damaged.

☐ **Celebrate Good Times—Come On!**
Take yourself out to dinner—you've made it!

A Place To Keep My Notes and Reminders…

29 Days to a Smooth Move
Make Your Own Moving Calendar

	Sunday	Monday	Tuesday	Wednesday	Thursday	Friday	Saturday
Let's get started!							
Make hay while the sun shines!							
Do these things before it gets hectic!							
Take care of the rest of the best!							
The crunch is on— and the end is in sight!							

A Place To Keep My Notes and Reminders...

Bonus

Just the Facts!

29 Days to a Smooth Move: Just the Facts! is a collection of Make a Moving Memos, Make a Dates and other materials from the book *29 Days to a Smooth Move.*

Use this section if you want to get "right to the writing" of your moving vitals and keep them in one place.

Section One

Save Scads of Your Time

This section of 29 Days to a Smooth Move *details how you can save time through planning, moving options and exploring your new community.*

My "Big Picture" To-Do List
(Overall moving priorities from A to Z, such as selling the house, packing, transferring the kids' school records)

_____

_____

_____

_____

_____

_____

_____

_____

_____

_____

_____

_____

_____

_____

_____

_____

_____

_____

The things I dread doing—and when they will be done!

Task   Date for Completion

_____

_____

_____

_____

_____

_____

_____

_____

_____

_____

The friends who can help with sorting, packing and more:

_____

_____

_____

_____

_____

_____

_____

_____

_____

People I know who may be able to recommend a mover:

_____

_____

_____

_____

_____

_____

_____

_____

_____

_____

Professional movers I plan to contact for estimates and/or questions:

_____

_____

_____

_____

_____

_____

_____

_____

_____

_____

_____

_____

My moving questions for the pros I may possibly hire:

_____

_____

_____

_____

_____

_____

_____

_____

_____

_____

Questions about insurance for the moving company:

_____

_____

_____

_____

_____

_____

_____

_____

_____

_____

At least three truck rental companies and their estimates:

Company   Estimate

_____

_____

_____

_____

_____

_____

_____

_____

_____

Questions for the truck rental or moving companies:

_____

_____

_____

_____

_____

_____

_____

_____

_____

Resources to gather from my new community

___ Newspaper

___ Penny Saver

___ Telephone book

___ Real estate guides

___ Book of Lists

Other:

_____

_____

_____

_____

_____

_____

_____

_____

_____

_____

Internet resources to surf:

WeatherChannel.com
USAToday.com

_____

_____

_____

_____

_____

_____

_____

_____

_____

_____

Questions for my child's new school:

_____

_____

_____

_____

_____

_____

_____

_____

_____

_____

_____

Section Two

Save Your Cents

This section of 29 Days to a Smooth Move *details how you can save money in packing and at tax time.*

In my new community, the average cost of:

Rent

_____

_____

Utilities

_____

_____

Cable

_____

_____

Gasoline

_____

_____

Groceries

_____

_____

Insurance

_____

_____

Gym

_____

_____

Other

_____

_____

_____

_____

_____

_____

The items I can deduct from my taxes:

_____

_____

_____

_____

_____

_____

_____

_____

_____

I Need It	*29 Days to a Smooth Move* Budgeting Worksheet	Estimate $	Actual $
	Description		
	MOVERS		
☐	Professional movers		
☐	Truck rental		
☐	Gas for rental		
☐	Additional mileage expenses		
☐	Hand truck/dolly		
☐	Furniture pads		
☐	OTHER:		
	PACKING SUPPLIES		
☐	3-ring binder		
☐	Black markers		
☐	Boxes with cell kits		
☐	Bubble wrap		
☐	Cat (or dog) carrier		
☐	Clear sealing tape and dispenser		
☐	Dish pack boxes		
☐	Electronics boxes		
☐	File storage boxes		
☐	Fireproof safe deposit box		
☐	Fragile labels		
☐	Furniture pads		
☐	Inkless newsprint		
☐	Lampshade boxes		
☐	Linen boxes		
☐	Mattress bags		
☐	Packing peanuts		
☐	Picture/mirror boxes		
☐	Room inventory labels		
☐	Twine		
☐	Utility knife		
☐	Wardrobe boxes		
☐	OTHER:		
	CLEANING SUPPLIES		
☐	Dumpster rental		
☐	Carpet cleaning service		
☐	Cleanser		
☐	Contractor garbage bags		
☐	Sponges/Scouring pads		
☐	Towels and rags		
☐	Professional cleaning service		
☐	OTHER:		

	MOVING OUT		
☐	Balance of rent on apartment		
☐	Lost security deposits on apartment		
☐	Home repair/selling preparation costs		
☐	Home closing costs		
☐	Balance of mortgage		
☐	OTHER:		

	GETTING THERE		
☐	Plane tickets		
☐	Auto inspection		
☐	Rental car		
☐	Gas for road trip		
☐	Lodging en route		
☐	Food		
☐	Entertainment		
☐	Auto Emergency Fund		
☐	OTHER:		

	SETTLING IN		
☐	Rental car		
☐	Grocery shopping		
☐	Household items		
☐	Toiletries		
☐	Vehicle registration		
☐	Driver's license application fee		
☐	New suit for job hunting		
☐	Security deposit		
☐	First month's rent		
☐	Deposit on home		
☐	OTHER:		

	SETTING UP UTILITIES/SERVICES		
☐	Cable/Satellite service		
☐	Cell phone service		
☐	Electric		
☐	Fuel/Gas		
☐	Gym membership		
☐	Internet service provider		
☐	Newspaper subscriptions		
☐	Sewer/Trash/Refuse		
☐	Telephone service		
☐	Water		
☐	OTHER:		

Description	Estimate $	Actual $
MY MISCELLANEOUS ITEMS		
**GRAND TOTAL		

Section Three

Save Your Securities

This section of 29 Days to a Smooth Move *details how you can make the most when selling your home, save the most when leaving your apartment and have peace of mind knowing that everyone from the babysitter to the beautician has been told of your move.*

The date the house is going on the market:

_____.

My asking price for the house:

_____.

Other homes for sale in my neighborhood:

Address   Listed Price

_____

_____

_____

_____

_____

_____

_____

_____

_____

_____

Must-do house projects before the house goes up for sale:

Room/Location   **Task**

_____

_____

_____

_____

_____

_____

_____

_____

_____

_____

_____

_____

_____

_____

Preshowing Checklist

You've done all the basic cleaning, but before you have that open house, take a run through your place and look for (or hide):

Dirty dishes
Soap scum in the sink
Inspection-friendly toilets
Paw prints on the kitchen floor
Damp towels
Dust in sunny places
Odd smells

List your own home's peculiarities (such as a faucet that has to be shut off extra hard not to drip) and things you don't want to notice when potential buyers are coming up the walk:

_____

_____

_____

_____

_____

_____

_____

_____

_____

_____

_____

_____

_____

_____

_____

Leaving the apartment to-do list:

Apartment manager notified of moving day.

Day _____ Time _____

____ Elevator/moving van parking space scheduled.

Walk through with manager set.

Day _____ Time _____

Other stuff to shiny up or schedule before leaving my digs:

_____

_____

_____

_____

_____

_____

_____

_____

_____

_____

_____

_____

_____

_____

_____

_____

Utilities To Cancel

Whether you're a homeowner or a renter, you'll need to do due diligence with your utility companies before moving on. Plan ahead with this worksheet, so the next occupant's water bill doesn't spill in your lap.

Utility	Phone #	Call Date	Confirmation #
Gas			
Fuel			
Electric			
Water			
Sewer			
Trash/Refuse			
Telephone			
Cell Phone			
Answering Service			
Cable			
Satellite TV			
Internet Service Provider			
Cable Modem Provider			
OTHER			
OTHER			
OTHER			

Also start notifying government offices, your service providers and banks!

Office	Phone #	Call Date	Confirmation #
Veterans Admin.			
Library			
City Hall			
Tax Assessor			
DMV			
Social Sec. Admin.			
State/Fed. Income Tax Bureaus			
OTHER			
OTHER			
OTHER			

Service Provider	Phone #	Call Date	Confirmation #
Accountant			
Beautician			
Chiropractor			
Dentist			
Doctors			
Financial Planner			
Handyman			
Insurance Agents			
Lawn Service			
Lawyer			

Manicurist	
Masseuse	
Pool Service	
Real Estate Agent	
Snow Service	
Stock Broker	
Water Softener Service	
OTHER	
OTHER	

Office	Phone #	Call Date	Confirmation #
AAA			
Agencies you donate to (United Way, Red Cross)			
Auto Service Station			
Banks			
Book/CD Clubs			
Credit Cards			
Credit Union			
Dry Cleaner			
Fine Dining Clubs			
Fitness Club			
Florists			
Lien Holders			
Mortgage Company			
Pharmacy			
Places you volunteer			
Schools/Colleges			
Video Stores			
Wine & Cheese Clubs			
OTHER			
OTHER			
OTHER			

Publication	Phone #	Call Date	Confirmation #
Alumni Newsletters			
Church Bulletin			
Fashion Catalogs			
Magazines			
Newspapers			
Trade Publications			
OTHER			
OTHER			
OTHER			

Utilities to Connect at Your New Residence

This list looks similar to the one you completed before you left your old place. Well, it's back—and you need it again if you don't want to finish this book by candlelight.

Utility	Phone #	Call Date	Confirmation #
Gas			
Fuel			
Electric			
Water			
Sewer			
Trash/Refuse			
Telephone			
Cell Phone			
Answering Service			
Cable			
Satellite TV			
Internet Service Provider			
Cable Modem Provider			
OTHER			
OTHER			
OTHER			

Section Four

Save Your Spine

This section of 29 Days to a Smooth Move *gets down and dirty on the specifics of packing and your physical move.*

The hardest items I have to pack and possible solutions:

_____

_____

_____

_____

_____

_____

_____

_____

_____

_____

_____

_____

_____

_____

_____

I have to return stuff to:

Person   Item

_____

_____

_____

_____

_____

_____

_____

_____

_____

_____

I have to collect my stuff from:

Person   Item

_____

_____

_____

_____

_____

_____

_____

_____

_____

_____

_____

Cleaning supplies I need to get the job done:

_____

_____

_____

_____

_____

_____

_____

_____

_____

_____

My most precious possessions that will not be boarding the moving van:

_____

_____

_____

_____

_____

_____

_____

_____

_____

_____

To-Do lists for having a garage sale:

Sale date(s) and time: _____

Rain date: _____

Location: _____

Friends and family I'll ask to join in on the garage sale:

Person   **Response**

_____

_____

_____

_____

_____

_____

_____

_____

_____

_____

_____

_____

_____

_____

_____

My sale's "hot items" to promote:

_____

_____

_____

_____

_____

_____

_____

_____

_____

_____

People I can borrow tables from:

_____

_____

_____

_____

_____

_____

_____

_____

_____

_____

Advertising

___ Fliers posted in grocery store (Week before sale)

___ Classified ad placed (To appear a few days before sale)

___ Signs hung (Day before sale)

Materials for "Check Out"

___ Change box (or fanny pack)
___ Change
___ Calculator
___ Bags
___ Paper
___ Pen

Other things to prepare/have on hand for the garage sale:

_____

_____

_____

_____

_____

_____

_____

_____

_____

_____

_____

Moving Day Lists

Not everything should board the bus!

Items not to be packed and/or let out of my sight:

_____

_____

_____

_____

_____

_____

_____

_____

_____

_____

_____

_____

_____

My moving out day is:

_____

When the movers will be at the house to move my stuff:

_____

Window of delivery when my movers will arrive at the new house:

_____

Moving day jobs and who gets to do what:

Job   Person

_____

_____

_____

_____

_____

_____

_____

_____

_____

Food items to have on hand for Moving Day:

Item   Phone number (order in!)

_____

_____

_____

_____

_____

_____

_____

_____

_____

_____

Large pieces of furniture and where each piece will reside:

Item   Room

_____

_____

_____

_____

_____

_____

_____

_____

_____

_____

Section Five

Save Your Sanity

This section of 29 Days to a Smooth Move *looks at the emotion commotion that accompanies moving. Move your pets and kids without tearing your hair out and stop and say goodbye to all you've known. Finally, dream a little dream about what good things are going to happen next!*

Identify the feelings you have about your move:

I feel...

_____

_____

_____

_____

_____

_____

Identify the positives and negatives about your move:

I'm happy about moving because:

_____

_____

_____

_____

_____

_____

"I'm not so thrilled" and maybe feeling blue about these aspects:

_____

_____

_____

_____

_____

My moving hang-ups and possible solutions:

_____

_____

_____

_____

How I will announce my move to friends and family:

_____

_____

_____

_____

For my goodbye ceremonies, I will:

_____

_____

_____

_____

_____

_____

Lists For Leaving Your Job

Date to give notice: _____

Exit interview: _____

Last day on the job: _____

Things to return to my soon-to-be former workplace:

_____

_____

_____

_____

_____

_____

Things of mine to retrieve from my workplace:

_____

_____

_____

_____

_____

_____

Last, but not least, the pets!

Vet checklist:

___ Records

___ Vaccinations

___ Treatments

___ Tranquilizers

The airlines I'm considering and their pet rules:

_____

_____

_____

_____

_____

_____

BONUS

Make Your House Your Home

Bummer! We're sorry to hear that you weren't selected to be the next guest on TLC's *Trading Spaces*.

Not to fret. With these helpful decorating and cozying up tips, your space will be the envy of the neighbors—not the product of their work—in less time than it takes Paige Davis to say "Time's up!"

Home Sweet Home?

Whether you find yourself standing in the middle of your pre-fab cookie cutter apartment with pseudo-wood cupboards or in the middle of a turn-of-the-century farmhouse with amenities that live up to its name—on the verge of tears—don't push the panic button just yet.

We know you just blew your wad getting to your new pad, but the inexpensive tips and tricks to follow are sure to have you feeling at home in no time.

10 Ways to Get Homey On a Budget

1. **Flowers in the Attic**
   Wondering what lies beyond the trap door? Don't waste a minute! Up, up and away with the boxes. We can't emphasize enough how important it is to unpack and remove the evidence of your trek. Even if household items aren't in their permanent positions, with the boxes out of sight, you'll feel less stress and more settled.

Donna's Ditty—

Boxes Be Gone!

If you've been following along, you've probably picked up on the fact that, unlike the dynamo that Tara is, I can be a bit of a procrastinator. An organized procrastinator, but a procrastinator. The best thing I did to make my new house a home is have my friend Daniel climb up into the generous crawl space my house offers and put away about a dozen of the boxes of things I wouldn't be needing right away.

Out of sight, out of mind—but it's a more relieved mind!

---

2. **Memories, Like the Corner of My Mind...**

    Scattered pictures, of the way we were. Yep, scatter those photographs. No doubt you're feeling a touch of homesickness about now. Ease the pain by spreading photos of your family, your goodbye parties and happy times around your place. The best part about framed photos is that they can be easily rearranged on tables, dressers and the fridge—without traumatizing the plasterboard. Use this decorating band-aid as temporary relief until you know where you want to pound holes for your larger artwork.

3. **Feed Me Seymour**

    Don't underestimate the power of plants! Nothing livens up a room more than our chlorophyll-filled friends. With just $25, you can fill your digs with dirt and greens in inexpensive terra cotta pots. Feeling especially creative? Why not bring the terra cotta to life with some paint? The art therapy might do you, and your windowsills, some good!

4. **Nurse...Scalpel Please!**

    You're not living in an operating room—turn down the lights! You may be tempted to settle for the glaring overhead fluorescents until you finalize furniture arrangements and position the mood lighting. Buy some bulbs and put your table and floor lamps to use. The ambient lighting will make your rooms appear smaller and cozier. Keep decorative nightlights a-glow and try a mini lamp on your cupboards to create that "we'll-leave-a-light-on-for-you" appeal.

5. **Curtain Call**

What's the number one tip the experts recommend to give your rooms character? Whether you call them curtains, window treatments or drapery, get hanging. Curtains are to windows as eyebrows are to faces…do you get our point here? Even if you're not sure of your color scheme yet, pick up some versatile and inexpensive rods, and be creative! Wrap cut fabric around the poles, drape linen napkins, start sewing or go neutral. Your windows will love you for it!

Tara's Tale—

Six Bright Smiles

When we moved into our house in Las Vegas, I took one look at the six huge windows in the living room and nearly tossed my cookies. I knew it would cost hundreds of dollars to dress the windows the way I wanted. I didn't waste a stitch of time devising my plan to outsmart the drapery companies. After getting ideas at home stores, I created a pattern, paid a visit to the discount fabric store and a roll of thread and—$86 and a few hours later—I had my perfect curtains, complete with matching tassels!

---

6. **Smoke…**

Ever wonder why people light so many candles in their homes around the holidays? To bring that warm feeling to the hearth of the home no doubt! Show off your personal style with simple votives, hurricanes, floating figures, or funk-a-delic varieties to add intimacy year round. No matter what wick you pick, keep them away from those curtains that you just put up!

7. **…And Mirrors**

It's true what they say—make a small space double in size with the help of mirrors. Prop them or pound them. Group them or let a grand one go it alone. We also hear it's good feng shui to have a house filled with mirrors—to reflect the positive energy. ("Feng what" you say? Don't worry, just get the mirrors.)

8. **Paint to Pillows**

   Feeling bold? Express yourself with a fresh palette for the walls.

   It takes patience to color-coordinate a home, but with a little help from those cute paint chips at your local home improvement store, you'll be seeing the rainbow of possibilities in no time!

   And painting isn't what it used to be. Choose one accent wall and paint it a bold color, leaving the others white. Roll, rag, stencil, texturize, faux finish, or antique to boost the WOW factor! Remember, dark paint creates a smaller space and light hues open up the walls.

   Once you're done, accessorize with pillows of all shapes and sizes. Paint and pillow to get almost instant gratification—and mileage from your wallet.

Tara's Tale—

Rollin', Rollin', Rollin'!

Ron and I have always been huge fans of colorful rooms. We weren't in our new house but three days before we were rolling our way to an apple-green family room and kitchen. Although it probably wasn't the most ideal time to paint (our to-do list was LONG), it was easy because everything had just been cleaned, no curtains existed and the walls were bare. A gallon of instant gratification goes a long way to make your house your home.

---

9. **Flush Away Dinginess**

   Don't kid yourself. Remodeling the bathroom will cost big bucks and big energy. But, *redecorating* the bathroom is a different story altogether! Rip down the water-damaged wallpaper, slap on a fresh coat of paint, invest in a decorative shower curtain and matching towels, replace the rusty towel rack, hide unsightly sink pipes with a "sink skirt" and frame the chipped mirror with colored tile chips. Why not add some life with plants? They're perfect for the greenhouse environment that is your bathroom!

Donna's Ditty—

On Deck

My landlord had taken the trouble to put in new paneling around my home's shower—except the paneling wasn't waterproof! I watched in dismay as mildew started to take over the crevices in between the squares in a matter of months.

Since I rent, my options were limited, however I decided a coat of paint couldn't hurt. After taking "before" pictures in case there was any question of what I did would hurt the home's value, I swabbed on waterproof white deck paint over the paneling.

Perfecto! My shower is now waterproof and clean looking. With a little ingenuity, you too can cover up some of your new home's blemishes.

10. Your Boudoir Beckons

It's time for pillow talk, but your bedroom is filled with noise…clutter…everything that doesn't "go" somewhere else. In the early days in your new community, there's nothing more important than a good night's sleep. Make your bedroom your sanctuary. Fill it with your favorite things and go ahead, it's time for some fresh flowers! You will only be as relaxed as your bedroom, so make its appearance (and feel) a priority.

Make a Moving Memo

The quick and easy projects I can do to cozy my home:

_____

_____

_____

_____

_____

_____

_____

_____

_____

_____

_____

_____

_____

BONUS

De-Stress For New Success

Settling Down

One thing you definitely need to get rid of (along with that Encyclopedia Britannica set from 1972) is some stress in your life.

We know what you're thinking: Tell me something I don't know!

Then you probably know that the difference between "knowing" something and "doing" something about it are two entirely different things.

But even though you have a million things in your mover's mind, you have to make room for one more thing—scheduling some timeout for yourself before, during and after your move.

In *29 Days to a Smooth Move* we talked a lot about packing a "morning after" box filled with supplies you'll need for the first night and day in your new home.

You can create the same concept to help yourself out physically and in spirit.

Some items to include in an emotional first aid kit:

A Real Kit!

While you're packing, set one box aside for your favorite pictures, inspirational book, candles, bubble bath—whatever calms you down in times of stress. And when the feeling of panic hits, take a deep breath, rummage through your box and pick out something to relax you for a few minutes.

Repeat After Me—I Have It All Together

There's a reason people tout positive affirmations—they work! Say to yourself several times a day:

"I face my future with a confident spirit."

"Let go and let be."

"I invite smooth transitions into my life."

Put the concepts out in the universe and look on in amazement as they come true!

Meditation and Visualization tapes

Put the packing or unpacking aside, sit back and listen to the sounds of the ocean or a positive speaker, such as Tony Robbins or Wayne Dyer. They will help you suppress anxieties and rev up your adventurous side.

20 Minutes a Day—Just For You

Maybe you want to pound out your frustrations on the treadmill or do some relaxing yoga or Qi Gong movements. Whatever you choose for your personal retreat, commit to it. You'll become more comfortable with yourself first, and your surroundings second.

Reach Out and Touch Someone

Keep the phone numbers of friend and family handy so you can call them one of them up when you really need to talk to a familiar voice. Or laugh with a familiar voice. Or have some familiar ears listen to you. Bonus points if you have a friend who moved recently and can commiserate!

Donna's Ditty—

Help Me, Tara!

Tara and I worked together in Erie. When I was debating my move to California I visited her cube frequently to discuss plans, hopes and dreams. She was a true blue friend and tireless personal cheerleader helping me through the turmoil of moving.

Six months to the day I left Pennsylvania, Tara and Ron started their own westward trek to Las Vegas. Although I wasn't there for her in person, we burned up the phone and Internet wires talking about their challenges and, Lady Luck being with us, now take advantage of the fact that Las Vegas is only a five-hour drive from San Diego.

The moral of the ditty? No matter how hectic things get, make the time to keep in touch with at least one "true blue" friend to share your moving misery and double your juxtaposed joy.

Settling In—For Good!

It's good to "become one" with your new home in spirit. Honor it. Play your favorite music as you unpack. Make your favorite meal in the new kitchen. Arrange pictures or furniture in one place so it looks familiar. It's a balm to the unsettled mover's soul.

"I'm Not Lost—I'm Exploring!"

Okay, the house is starting to look like home—what's outside those windows?

Checking out your new community can be a lot of fun if you make it so.

Whether you're a country mouse moving to the big city or a city slicker going rustic, it's time to get out and explore! Where will you buy groceries? Gas? How far to the kids' school? Where's the hardware store? Any quiet little eateries around? Is it going to be the gym or walks on long winding roads? All these questions, and more, can be answered by touring your new community.

And the fun part of it is that it doesn't have to be done in one day—you can take your time and make your new surroundings—and community—a home.

If a job search is in the works, we have a book for that, too!

Peruse the table of contents and read the first chapter of our book: *Get A Job! Put Your Degree To Work.* If you like what you see, you can find the rest at getajobbook.com.

Get A Job!
Put Your Degree To Work

Table of Contents

Chapter 7
Details, Details, Details
Do it right and check it twice.

Chapter 8
All Aboard: Career Services
Uncover the best-kept secret on campus!

Chapter 9
Doin' the Hand Jive
Get a grip on your body language.

Chapter 10
Suit Up For Success
Look the part and land the job.

Chapter 11
The Art of the Interview
Prepare yourself to handle questions with ease.

Chapter 12
Company Calling!
Strike just the right tone in a telephone interview.

Chapter 13
Application Know How
Fill in the blanks and find yourself employed.

Chapter 14
The Non-Interview Interview
Come in the back door with an informational interview.

Chapter 15
Tote 'n' Totables
Take these accessories to bolster your interviewing impression.

Chapter 16
Being Dined Without the Wine
Dish out your best during a mealtime interview.

Chapter 17
Talking Turkey
Negotiate a salary you can live with—and on.

Chapter 18
It Ain't Easy Being Green
Survive your first day on the job!

Appendix

Contract For A Successful Job Search
If you want to make it happen, put it in writing.

Job Lead Forms
Keep track of all your efforts.

Sample Cover Letters
Take a memo or two as we show you how it's done!

Sample Resumes
Objective: To give you some format and wording ideas.

Sample Thank You Letters
Ways to say "Dear Future Employer, I think you are swell!"

Chapter 1

Create a Job-Finding Command Center

Establish an organized place to keep your pens, paper and printer.

Finding a job after graduation takes a lot of energy. You'll be scanning the classi-fieds, surfing the Web, creating resumes, composing cover letters and preparing for interviews. Save your energy for completing those tasks with business-like poise instead of spending time shuffling through piles looking for pens, searching for highlighters and playing "find the stapler."

Donna's Ditty—

What? Me Organized?

More than a few of my friends are snickering as they read this because my desk frequently resembles a war zone. When I was a writer and editor at a large east coast insurer, one of my co-workers used to bring visitors over just to marvel at the sight of my workstation and its sea of empty water bottles, overflow of paper (my own "layer method" of filing) and rainbow of scrawled upon Post-It Notes.

But even I admit that I work better when I follow my own advice about the merits of keeping a neat and clean desk. When I do, I'm more productive and creative—things get done better and faster. (In my defense, you should see the way I keep folders and files organized on my PC—one click and you'd find the rest of this chapter lickity-split!)

Here's a Bright Idea

Do only job-finding activities in your command post. It's not the area to stack used textbooks or dirty laundry. Dedicating this space to finding employment will keep you focused on the task at hand.

Create a Job-Finding Command Center

Establish a place to keep your pens, paper and printer.

Ready a Space

Find a place to set up your job-finding command center and consolidate all your job search materials at this one easy and convenient post. Your computer desk is an ideal spot, but you'll also need an offline filing systems for papers and resumes. Other possible locations include a kitchen table, a card table, a spare bedroom or even a milk crate (the legal ones, please!).

Set Up Shop

Stock your space with all the necessities (we've provided a list below to get you started). A trip to Office Depot or Staples will probably be in order, but try to stick with only the items you definitely need and can carry to the car in one trip. That mahogany roll-top desk with the 24K gold filing cabinet would be cool, but you're not employed yet!

Take Out the Trash

Incorporate some daily and weekly de-cluttering activities in your routine, including vacuuming the floor, dusting equipment, sponging off coffee mug rings and taking out the trash. Do the same with your computer files—electronic pages you no longer need weigh you and your job search down.

Keep a Calendar

Your planner, your friend. If you don't already have a daily planner, get one. One with an hourly breakdown works well so you can jot down meetings with contacts, application due dates, your interview times, reminders to follow up on resumes and more. Many e-mail systems also offer decent calendar programs. The key is to develop a reliable system you will use.

Who's In Your Little Black Book?

Along with a dependable time management system, you also need a plan for keeping track of your growing network of contacts. It's not uncommon to leave a networking event with dozens of business cards. One idea is to jot down a few items describing the person who gave you the card right on the card itself. It'll jog your memory days later when otherwise you'd be looking at it blankly muttering, "Who was this again?" You can then put the name and contact information in an address book, e-mail program or slip it right into a Rolodex.

Top of the To Do List

Develop a system for creating and keeping track of lists. You'll have a lot of them, such as ones for needed office supplies, want ads calling your name and a growing number of "must do" activities. Use a certain color sticky pad, unique notebook or easy-to-access computer file.

 ## Smart Thinking

Put this information to work and create your own job search center. Stock your center with the tools you need to keep organized and on task. Supply suggestions include:

Address Book or Rolodex	Filing System	Resume Paper
Appointment Calendar	Highlighter	Space to Work
Business Cards	Pens	Stationary
Business Envelopes	Postage Stamps	Trashcan with Shredder

Thank You Cards (elegant and conservative—no bears or bunnies)

 ## Power It Up!

Organize and file papers in your job search center at least once a week. Update your calendar and planner, throw out the no longer useful, etc. A good time to do your weekly makeover is Sunday night so you can start the new week off in the right light—all spruced up and ready for success!

Straight from the Experts

"You can exercise a remarkable amount of control over your career destiny if you are willing to take responsibility for it. Every decision you make during your undergraduate years has career implications. The friends you make, the major you choose, the elective courses you take, the extracurricular activities you participate in, the minor you choose, the professors you befriend, the summer jobs you work and the ways you spend your leisure time.

"We believe your career future is too important to leave to chance. Start on the very first day of classes of your freshmen year to maximize your career opportunities."

> Jack Rayman, Ph.D.
> Director, Career Services
> Affiliate Professor, Counseling Psychology & Education
> Penn State University, University Park, Pa.

"Early preparation is the key. Research the company, have your resume always updated, secure letters of recommendation and dress professionally to be competitive and marketable."

> Robert J. Hvezda
> Director of Career Services and Internship Programs
> Office of Career Services and Internship Programs
> Mercyhurst College, Erie, Pa.

About the Authors

It was the ultimate challenge…who would settle in the sunshine first? Would it be Donna and her cats or Tara and her husband Ron?

Fourt years later, the ultimate challenge is but a moving memory (although Donna will never forget that she made it to San Diego six months to the day before Tara and Ron showed up in Las Vegas!). Now business partners and best buds to boot, Donna and Tara share more than moving memories of their home-town, Erie, Pa.—they've shared a passion for writing and reliving the trials and triumphs of their cross-country moves—so yours can be just as smooth.

Kozik is based in San Diego and holds a Master's of Business Administration (MBA) degree with a concentration in marketing. Maras lives in Las Vegas and has a Master's Degree in Communication Studies from University of Nevada Las Vegas.

Owners of a book writing and publishing business, Kozik and Maras are the authors of *Get A Job! Put Your Degree To Work*, a go-to job finding resource for the recent or soon-to-be college graduate. Check it out at getajobbook.com.

Thinking about getting married in Las Vegas?

Look for *The Las Vegas Wedding Advisor*, Tara and Donna's next book, to be published in Spring 2006. From chapels to dresses to transportation, *The Las Vegas Wedding Advisor* is your personal wedding consult to the ins and outs of saying "I do" in Las Vegas.

Find out more at **lasvegasweddingadvisor.com**

29DaysToASmoothMove.com
info@29DaysToASmoothMove.com

Marik Communications LLC
2828 University Ave. # 227
San Diego CA 92104
USA

978-0-595-35957-8
0-595-35957-4

Printed in the United States
105798LV00007B/54/A